Anonymous

Course of Study for the Public Schools of the District of Columbia

Together with the Rules governing the Schools

Anonymous

Course of Study for the Public Schools of the District of Columbia
Together with the Rules governing the Schools

ISBN/EAN: 9783337157531

Printed in Europe, USA, Canada, Australia, Japan

Cover: Foto ©ninafisch / pixelio.de

More available books at **www.hansebooks.com**

COURSE OF STUDY

FOR THE

PUBLIC SCHOOLS

OF THE

DISTRICT OF COLUMBIA,

TOGETHER WITH THE

RULES GOVERNING THE SCHOOLS.

Adopted October 1, 1892.

WASHINGTON, D. C.:
BYRON S. ADAMS, PRINTER AND PUBLISHER,
1892.

REFERENCE TABLE.

	PAGE.
Names of Members of the Board of School Trustees	3
Officers of the Board	3
Standing Committees	5
Directions to Teachers	7
Language	9
Number	35
Algebra	43
Geography	45
U. S. History	72
General Remarks on the Study of Nature	79
Plant Work	82
Animal Work	91
Physiology	98
Physics	108
Penmanship	111
Drawing	114
Work in Shops	156
Cooking	157
Sewing	157
Music	159
Health Exercises	165
High School (in detail)	178
High School Courses Outlined	189
Business High School	190
Normal Training Schools	192
Appendixes	193
Rules	213

REFERENCE TABLE BY GRADES.

FIRST YEAR.

Language	16
Number	35
Plant Work	82
Animal Work	91
Physiology	98
Penmanship	111
Drawing	114
Music	160
Health Exercises	171

SECOND YEAR.

	PAGE.
Language	19
Number	35
Plant Work	84
Animal Work	92
Physiology	100
Penmanship	111
Drawing	120
Music	160
Health Exercises	171

THIRD YEAR.

Language	22
Number	35
Geography	45
Plant Work	87
Animal Work	93
Physiology	101
Penmanship	112
Drawing	127
Sewing	157
Music	161
Health Exercises	173

FOURTH YEAR.

Language	23
Number	35
Geography	54
Plant Work	89
Animal Work	95
Physiology	102
Penmanship	112
Drawing	133
Sewing	158
Music	162
Health Exercises	173

FIFTH YEAR.

Language	26
Number	37
Geography	63
U. S. History	72
Physiology	103

	PAGE.
Penmanship	112
Drawing	138
Sewing	158
Music	163
Health Exercises	174

SIXTH YEAR.

Language	27
Number	38
Geography	66
U. S. History	73
Physiology	104
Penmanship	112
Drawing	144
Sewing	158
Music	163
Health Exercises	174

SEVENTH YEAR.

Language	29
Number	41
Geography	67
U. S. History	75
Physics	108
Penmanship	113
Drawing	147
Bench Work (boys)	156
Cooking (girls)	157
Music	164
Health Exercises	175

EIGHTH YEAR.

Language	32
Number and Algebra	43
Geography	70
Physiology	106
Penmanship	113
Drawing	151
Bench Work (boys)	156
Cooking (girls)	157
Music	164
Health Exercises	175

HIGH SCHOOLS.

ACADEMIC HIGH SCHOOL.

	PAGE.
Mathematics	178
Chemistry, Mineralogy, Physics	179
Zoölogy, Botany	180
Geology, History and Political Science	181
English	182
German, Latin	183
Greek, Drawing	184
Vocal Music, Manual Training, Military Drill	186
Library, Text Books	187
Courses of Study Outlined	189

BUSINESS HIGH SCHOOL. 190

NORMAL TRAINING SCHOOLS.
(Page 192.)

BOARD OF TRUSTEES OF PUBLIC SCHOOLS, DISTRICT OF COLUMBIA.

Name.	Term Expires.	Address.
LOCAL COMMITTEES.		
First Division.		
J. J. DARLINGTON, LL. D...	September 13, 1895........	410 Fifth street, northwest.
Second Division.		
LEONARD C. WOOD............	September 13, 1895........	507 E street, northwest.
Third Division.		
JAS. W. WHELPLEY, esq....	September 13, 1893........	Treasury Department.
Fourth Division.		
DAVID H. HAZEN, M. D......	September 13, 1893........	407 Sixth street, southwest.
Fifth Division.		
JOHN T. MITCHELL, esq....	September 13, 1893........	1339 F street, northwest.
Sixth Division.		
A. H. WITMER, M. D............	September 13, 1893........	St. Elizabeth Insane Asylum.
F. J. SHADD, M. D................	September 13, 1894.......	Freedmen's Hospital.
Seventh Division.		
BLANCHE K. BRUCE............	September 13, 1895........	City Hall.
Eighth Division.		
L. A. CORNISH, esq...............	September 13, 1893........	Sixth Auditor's Office, Busch Bldg.

OFFICERS OF THE BOARD.

President,
JOHN T. MITCHELL, 1339 F street, northwest.

Secretary,
J. G. FALCK, Franklin School.

Superintendent of Schools,
W. B. POWELL, A. M., Franklin School.

Superintendent of Colored Schools,
G. F. T. COOK, A. M., Sumner School.

Meetings of the Board of Trustees.

The stated meetings of the Board of Trustees are held on the second Tuesday of each month, and also on the last Tuesday in June.

Standing Committees of the Board.

Rules.
Messrs. MITCHELL, WOOD, BRUCE.

Ways and Means, Supplies and Accounts.
Messrs. WHELPLEY, HAZEN, CORNISH.

Buildings, Repairs and Furniture.
Messrs. WOOD, WITMER, CORNISH.

Normal and High Schools.
Messrs. DARLINGTON, MITCHELL, BRUCE, WHELPLEY.

Teachers and Janitors.
Messrs. WITMER, WHELPLEY, SHADD.

Text-Books, Studies, Examinations, Promotions and Scholarships.
Messrs. HAZEN, MITCHELL, BRUCE.

Penmanship and Music.
Messrs. SHADD, WHELPLEY, HAZEN.

Industrial Education and Drawing.
Messrs. CORNISH, DARLINGTON, WOOD.

Library and Annual Report.
Messrs. WITMER, DARLINGTON, SHADD.

Course of Study.

To the Teacher:

The attention of the teacher is especially directed to rule 31, in the appendix of this volume.

It is as desirable for the teacher to know the condition of the

ERRATA:

On page 31, in the topic "Forms" in the outline of Verbs, insert the word "past" under the word "present."

On page 41, in "Tabular View," second column, eighth line, read "principal" instead of "principle."

On page 43, in the third line of the 6th paragraph, read "profitably" instead of "profitable."

On page 76, in the fourth line of the 10th paragraph, read "admission" instead of "administration."

busy teacher does not detect its presence until much of its evil work has been done.

Too often the teacher does not know, or is indifferent to the fact that the air of the school-room is impure. Every teacher should seek diligently to make himself sensitive to the presence of impurity in the atmosphere.

If the teacher would leave the room occasionally to breathe for a few moments an atmosphere known to be pure, on returning he would be able to discover the condition of the school-room air.

It is advised that teachers, at half-hour intervals, give the

Course of Study.

To the Teacher:

The attention of the teacher is especially directed to rule 31, in the appendix of this volume.

It is as desirable for the teacher to know the condition of the school-room, respecting warmth and purity of air, as it is that he should know the value of the recitation work of the pupil.

School-rooms are more frequently too hot than too cold.

When the school-room is found to be too warm, measures should be taken to lower the temperature at once. If to do this it is found necessary or desirable to open doors or windows, care should be taken that no pupil remains seated in a draft of cold air. It is advised that at such times the pupils be given the freedom of the school-room and allowed a brief time for recreation.

So quietly and gradually does impurity approach that the busy teacher does not detect its presence until much of its evil work has been done.

Too often the teacher does not know, or is indifferent to the fact that the air of the school-room is impure. Every teacher should seek diligently to make himself sensitive to the presence of impurity in the atmosphere.

If the teacher would leave the room occasionally to breathe for a few moments an atmosphere known to be pure, on returning he would be able to discover the condition of the school-room air.

It is advised that teachers, at half-hour intervals, give the systematized physical exercises—that are prescribed for their respective grades—not to occupy more than three, four or five minutes, at which time the air of the school-room should be changed by opening doors or windows, or both. This would change the air of the room often enough to insure comparative freedom from impurity, and besides, would give mental rest and physical recreation to the pupils.

Pupils should not be allowed to remain in school with wet feet. Pupils should not be sent away from school for any cause when the weather is inclement.

Language.

The following extracts are taken, with slight alterations, from the annual report for the year 1889-90 :

CORRECT LANGUAGE TEACHING THE PROPER PREPARATION FOR LEARNING TO READ.

The ultimate purpose of learning to read is to secure the training that will give its possessor the power to see the concrete as clearly in the written description as the trained eye would see the thing described; to feel the emotion expressed as his own ; to know the willing expressed or to understand the conclusions expressed, as if willing, doing, or making the conclusions himself.

Learning to read may be considered under two general heads :

First, learning the symbols in which the known is preserved.

Second, learning how to add to one's store of knowledge by studying these symbols in which the knowledge sought is formulated.

Or, to express the same in a different way—

First, learning to recognize the forms of speech—words, signs, idiom, sentences, discourse—symbols representing what is known, what is definitely in the mind of the learner.

Second, learning to get information from forms of speech—words, signs, idiom, sentences, discourse.

The more faithfully forms of speech represent correct ideas existing in the mind of the learner when he learns them, the better is he prepared for the second part of learning to read. Words or other signs, if learned as the symbols of imperfect or incorrect ideas, indefinite or false relations, will ever after be misleading, or, when their true meanings have become known, will ever need to be translated when used.

The child's first effort in learning to read, if Nature's laws are to guide in the work, must be to recognize his own words, representing his own knowing, his own thinking, his own feeling, his own willing, his own concluding, his own doing. It is of the highest importance that these words stand for both correct ideas and exact ideas.

The vocabulary which the child brings to school does not, if a small percentage of words be excepted, represent exactness. A few names stand for the right things, whereas many or most of his words representing qualities, feelings, abstractions, are not the symbols in any degree of exactness of the ideas for which they really stand existing in his own mind, It is unwise to teach him these as symbols of what they now represent to him. It is unwise to characterize the beginnings of his school education by such indefiniteness or such obscurity.

The child, as a preparation for learning to read, must have exact ideas and thought, and must be made to express the same correctly and well. The wider the range of ideas, the more diversified the knowing and thinking consistent with sequence and unity, the more nearly they represent all the functions of the mind, however childlike their manifestations, the more rapidly and perfectly will the child appreciate the symbolic nature of words, seeing in them entities, living realities; the more rapidly will he learn to read, and the more delightful will learning to read be to him. With how great enjoyment does he see his own thought in graphic symbols of his own spoken words.

Not only, therefore, must the child think, and think correctly, but the teacher must know what he thinks and how he thinks, for under no other conditions can it be known that he speaks correctly and with exactness.

How soon in the average school work does the child learning to read reach a point in his progress where the reading matter is too difficult for him. The reason should be sought. The trouble is not that he can not be made to pronounce the words, for this can be accomplished, so thorough may be the school drill and so inevitable the mechanical results of prescribed processes. The reason is not far to seek. The words and sentences represent ideas and thoughts that have never had a lodgment in his mind; more than this, he has never learned symbols of corresponding ideas and thoughts by which these may be interpreted. Presistent drilling on such words as these will do little toward teaching the child to read.

Much reading of matter similar to that previously read in his progress does not prepare the child to advance satisfactorily. This has been demonstrated times without number by the addition of supplementary reading matter.

The studying of definitions given in the book will do little good. Definitions carefully given by an intelligent teacher will do little good. The child must be given experiences represented by the words he is to learn, or experiences similar to them. He must be trained in broader lines of seeing, of feeling, of planning and doing.

He must be led into the field of imagination and be made to create thought (on determinative lines). He must be exercised in fields of emotional activity, of loving, of hating, of being generous, of being cautious, of being fearful, and then he must be helped to express all these sensations or feelings, and must learn their symbols as the representatives of what exists in his own mind. With this preparation he can advance in learning to read.

The child must be made to know more, step by step, in advance of his learning to read, and what he reads at first must represent what he knows. These representations in his mind will be to him his true interpreters of what he afterwards reads on kindred subjects. They will be to him the key to the dictionary, making lists of synonymous words intelligible to him.

Knowing is the only safe compass and helmsman in the boundless and dangerous sea of emotional activity; knowing is the only source whence proceeds determinative, profitable, creative activity; knowing is the only reliable enginery of willing, whether it be concluding or doing.

Subjects of thought must be presented to the child first through the senses. He must be made to know through original channels of information.

The best possible work in exact seeing is the study of forms offered in exercises that come under the head of drawing. The lessons given under this head are, first, the modeling of the forms in clay in imitation of forms presented to the child. These lessons train his eye, his judgment, and his hand—coworkers for the accomplishment of a definite purpose. Then he must be carefully trained to talk about the forms he has made.

Other kinds of work under the head of drawing are sticklaying, paper-folding, and combining geometric forms in wood or in paper, all of which, after being made, should be represented with pencil, and in turn be described. Some of these may be compared and the processes of doing given, which is narration. It is thus seen that much exact language training is possible under the head of drawing.

Good work may be done simultaneously with the number lessons which take their start in the form lessons, in making simple problems and in solving them.

Much good work can be done for a short time by naming the objects in the room and stating their relative positions and some of their qualities, by the use of simple pictures for description and story, by making tableaux of children and their playthings for a like purpose.

The last-named subjects are soon exhausted without too much labor on the part of the teacher.

No other subject which the child can readily understand and which, at the same time, will be interesting to him, offers such opportunities for seeing, such opportunities for training in the exact use of a broad vocabulary, available for general purposes and to a limited extent possessed by the child, as the study of natural history and elementary physics.

Forms, sizes, colors; number, uses, positions, all offer opportunity for exact seeing, exact knowing, and exact expression.

Comparison of these offers opportunity for exact seeing of likenesses and differences, for intelligent conclusions, and for the exact expression of such seeing and concluding.

The amount of training which it is possible to give young children in correct, exact seeing; correct, exact thinking; in the early drawing lessons, in the early number lessons, and by the use of natural objects, plants, animals, and the human body, is very great. Material for such lessons, moreover, is very easily obtained and prepared by the teacher.

By the means indicated in the foregoing for inciting the child to thought and for directing him in his thinking, it is possible and easy to give the best training in the use of language, which training is the best possible, indeed the only proper preparation for learning to read.

It will therefore be seen that, whereas the study of elementary science educates by training the child's perceptions and his comparing and concluding faculties, as no other study can do at this stage of his education, and at the same time enriches his mind with knowledge, its introduction at this time is chiefly to furnish the means of accurate and determinative training in the English language; for the work is not done that the child may learn and recite facts, but it is done that he may see facts, and thus be led to use language for exact and correct expression.

This work, if properly done, is far-reaching in its educative effects, whether mind development or language training be its purpose; for objects must not be studied in a heterogeneous way, but should be presented in groups whose parts are related. For instance, if a leaf is studied, several kinds of leaves must be studied in connection therewith. These, by a perception of their differences, must be separated into groups, after which many leaves may be found by the child, each of which he, deciding for himself, must place in the proper group. If an animal (as the squirrel) is studied, two or more animals belonging to the group of gnawing animals must be studied also, that relations may be seen, comparisons may be made, and conclusions drawn therefrom.

There is, moreover, idiom of the English language that belongs to description; this the child gets by help of the teacher when he describes the thing examined. There is English idiom, used only in comparing; this the child gets and uses when making comparisons, when contrasting the objects considered. There is English idiom belonging to narration; this the child is helped to by the teacher, and uses when telling the story of the growth, of the life, or of the incidents of the capture, of finding, or of buying what he has examined, described and compared. Thus is his vocabulary enriched by idiom that will never be there as a possession except by some such means. Now when the child sees the word for the first time they are not meaningless to him; he greets them as friends whom he has neverbefore seen. The reading of good English with such preparation is not only easy to the child, but soon becomes a delight to him.

The lessons given under the head of physiology (laws of health and cleanliness) should be, so far as they relate to anatomy, the same kind of lessons as those given on plants and animals; but in so far as they relate to the laws of health, evil effects of narcotics, stimulants, etc., they must necessarily be more didactic in their character, but are at this stage of equal value to the child, for he has grown strong enough to receive profitably what is dictated to him.

In addition to the kinds of work above named, vapor, with its phenomena of steam, cloud, mist, fog, rain, hail, snow, are to be taught by experiment and objects as a beginning of the study of geography, as well as for the special purpose of language training and of properly preparing the child to read. In this subject is presented a kind of learning quite different from anything the child has had before, namely, discovering by experiment. Water under the influence of heat turns to steam, leaves the receiver, and for a moment is lost to sight, when, by the influence of cold, it returns to view as mist, and soon looks into his face from the side of an ice pitcher.

In the various parts of this interesting and most practicable work excellent opportunity is found for training the productive imagination in the exercise of creative functions of the mind in determinative lines, the foundation for which is securely laid in the many facts learned. As the child presents the supposed history or biography of a drop of water on the pane of glass, or other like subjects, the teacher can judge of the intelligence with which it is done, for he can estimate by known laws whether the imagination of the talker or writer is clear, healthy, and under control, or is clouded, unintelligent, undirected, or visionary. Such work broadens the vocabulary, gives subjects for conversation and composition, and prepares the child to read valuable literature on the different forms of vapor.

While the distinctive purpose of the teaching of reading in the first three grades of the school is to make the children know the symbols representing their own knowledge and mental processes, much practice must be given in reading the same and kindred facts and processes expressed by accepted authorities. This is done for broadening the vocabularies of the children and for teaching the kindred significance of words. Some reading is done to get information, similar to that in the possession of the children to be interpreted by it and assimilated with it.

Learning to read should do much toward training the attention and the judgment, which should result in conscious power. As in the preparation for learning to read the pupil learns to know and to feel his ability to investigate and to decide through original channels of information, so now he must gain a corresponding confidence in his ability, to investigate, to see, and to know through symbolic channels.

In the fourth grade the reading begins to be more distinctively for the purpose of getting information, and is more and more so characterized through the remaining grades.

Great care is required in the transition. For this purpose the text must be illustrated by objective work or by experiment, and should be supplemented by tests for truth and for application, the effort being to train the learner to see accurately and to know exactly by reading.

No greater care is required in any reading lesson than in those belonging to this transition period.

The historical story begun in the fifth grade can be understood only by examination of many objects representing the lives and customs of the people and times studied and by intelligent comparison of the same with corresponding objects representing the lives and customs of the people of to-day.

Objective work is all important in this grade of school, but its use is for another purpose than that for which it is given in the lower grades.

In whatever grade science lessons are given, groups or units of related objects should be given, by which unity and symmetry may be taught and, furthermore, these lessons should lead to or supplement or be made a means of practically applying some other part of the work of the grade. This illustrates the interdependence of the parts of this course of instruction.

Course in Language.

FIRST YEAR.

Seeing and Talking :

(No less than three months should be given to this unit of work.)

The chief purpose of this unit of work is to train pupils first to see groups or bodies of associate thought, and then to represent them as entireties in connected discourse.

The thought arranged must be furnished. The pupil must be led to see the thought and its arrangement, and then must be led, and if necessary helped, to express it as arranged in connected discourse.

The teacher must supply and teach the necessary composition idiom for the proper expression of relations that the children are made to see in the groups of thought presented.

The groups of thought presented at first must be very simple, and should become more complex by very easy steps. These groups of thought may be—

> Simple tableaux, arranged in the presence of the children, so that the arrangement may be seen as it takes place, the children in many instances helping to form them ;
> Simple pictures rapidly made in the presence of the children ;
> Parts of plants, as leaves, stems, roots, simple flowers (See outline of Plant Lessons) ;
> Familiar animals having marked characteristics, as the cat, the squirrel, the duck, the owl (See outline of Animal Lessons) ;
> Parts of the human body (See outline of Physiology work) ;

Geometric forms, made by modeling solids of clay or other plastic material ;*
Geometric forms made by laying sticks ;†
Geometric forms made by folding paper involving size and color ;‡
Other groups of thought, as a hat, a basket of fruit, a broken doll, etc.

The teacher should correct mispronunciation and false syntax, but not in such a way as to destroy unity of thought or to take the effort of the child from the chief purpose of the exercise—the expression of associate thought in connected discourse—the representation of what is seen.

After the children have acquired some ability to see simple entireties and the parts that make them, and have gained some power in the use of their vocabularies for the representation of what they see and want to express, they should begin to learn by sight the words they use in such composition ; that is, the children may begin to learn to read.

Reading :

At first, from the blackboard, words and short sentences from the children's own compositions may be taught, and soon larger compositions made by the children.

Do not allow the children to read disconnected matter, except as they are drilled for the rapid seeing of groups of related words—phrases and short sentences taken from the compositions made by the children themselves.

Let the teacher remember that if ever education should begin with the known, it is in learning to read. The known are the thoughts expressed by what is to be read, and the spoken language expressing it ; the unknown are the written symbols, words, signs, sentences. In all this beginning work, the teacher must be sure that there is a well-established known from which to lead.

The two Primers and the two First Readers, and from two to five times as much other matter made and written by the children, should be read the first year.

---

*See Appendix A. †See Appendix B. ‡See Appendix C.

Spelling:

All words used in writing.

The children must early master the sounds of the consonants and their combinations. In connection with word learning, the children should do some oral spelling.

Let the standard with the teacher and pupil at all times be perfection. Make children ashamed and unwilling to mispell with pen or pencil, as that is the whole secret of good spelling.

Composition Idiom:

While learning to express what they see, the children will need to use some or all of the following composition idioms, which, at the end of the year, should constitute a part of the vocabularies of the children available for speech or for written work. The children should acquire a discriminating use of these idioms in common speech.

Composition Idioms:

and	but	when	where	for	because	after
as soon as		after this	while	before		whereas
		who	which		whom	whose
			which		whom	whose
		from	"		"	"
		with	"		"	"
		for	"		"	"
		before	"		"	"
		on	"		"	"
		to	"		"	"
		about	"		"	"
		at	"		"	"

Participles taking the places of relative clauses, as: "The boy *standing* at the board is my brother."

Grammatic Idiom:

As the children grow in strength they should be led to see some forms of words, and to understand the meanings of such forms—what they represent.

The following are suggested:

The singular and plural forms:
   (a) Of some nouns whose plurals are made by the addition of *s* to the singular;
   (b) Of some nouns whose plurals are made by the addition of *es* to the singular;
   (c) Of a few nouns whose plurals are made by an internal change;

Also a few nouns used only in the plural.

The children may be taught:
1. The use of *is*, *are*, *was*, *were*, *has* and *have*;
1. The use of *this* and *these*; *that* and *those*;
3. The use of *a*, *an* and *the*;
4. The uses of some of the most common contracted forms of words.
5. The uses of the forms denoting present and past time of *see*, *go*, *draw*, *throw*, *ring*, *sing*, *do*, *write*, *blow*, *grow*, *know*, *break*.*

The pupils should learn by observation how to close the different kinds of sentences, and should learn as a part of their spelling how to begin sentences, and how to begin the proper names which they use, as well as how to write *I* and *O* as words.

SECOND YEAR.

Seeing, Talking and Writing:

Continue the work of training children to see and to express what they see in idiomatic English connectedly; that is, to make oral and written compositions, the thought and its arrangement being furnished in all cases. Subjects similar to

---

*The two forms of each verb should be taught by association and contrast: To-day I see; yesterday I saw, etc. The children should be able to write in columns the two forms of these verbs.

those suggested for the first year may be taken, but should be more difficult. (See outlines of Plant and Animal Work, and also Appendices A, B and C, second year.)

Much attention should be given to Narration. The children should be led to distinguish between descriptions and stories—groups of facts having space relations mainly, and groups of facts (acts) having time relations mainly.

Before children are asked to talk or to write—that is, to make compositions—be sure:

1st, That they see or know as an entirety the group of related facts which they are to describe or to relate;

2d, That their vocabularies contain the idiom necessary to express the relations of thought they will want to represent;

3d, That the children's purposive efforts be to describe what they see or to narrate a group of related events that they know, and not simply to say or to write something.

The greater part of the work of learning to talk well is that of thoroughly learning something to talk about. Forms of speech must indeed be learned but a knowledge of them and their uses comes easily to the mind that is full of something it wants to express.

The test of the teacher's success will be a growing desire, as well as an ability, on the part of the child to use language correctly for the expression of well-defined thought.

The children in this grade should be asked to describe only what they can see and examine while talking or writing. They should be asked to relate only those events that they have witnessed or experienced within a short time previous to their efforts at narration, or events that may be inferred by looking at a series of pictures on the blackboard or elsewhere. Plays to be acted in the school-room; the events of a recitation; the events of a half-hour in the school-room are suggested. The object of the work is to teach the children to use English correctly and for a purpose, and not to pass the time of a recitation in aimless, profitless talking, or in writing disconnected sentences.

Comparisons offer excellent opportunity to teach the correct and definite use of language. Some new idioms will be needed in this work. To teach these idioms is one important purpose of the work.

The comparative forms of adjectives and adverbs will be required. (See also composition idiom in first grade work.)

The work in comparison should be confined to objects that the children can see and handle. Avoid objects too nearly alike, and also objects in too great contrast to each other. Children will not readily see likenesses and differences between a leaf and a bird, but will see and can be made to talk methodically and accurately about the likenesses and differences between two birds that belong to different grand divisions of birds, or between two leaves that differ in form and structure, or two flowers belonging to different orders, or between a cat and a squirrel, two hats of different makes or styles, etc., etc.

Let the children *see* and tell in good English idiom what they see.

While learning to see things singly and in groups they should be led to see forms of speech that represent them and that represent what is said about them.

Practice should be given in reproducing short stories.

Grammatic Idiom:

The grammatic idiom of the first grade is to be reviewed and its use further developed and emphasized as the number of words known by sight increases. Teach the singular and plural forms—

1. Of some nouns ending in *y*.
2. Of some nouns ending in *f* or *fe*.
3. Of some nouns whose plurals are formed irregularly; as, *ox*, *oxen*.

Teach the children to distinguish between the plural form and the possessive singular form.

Reading:

The two Second Readers, a part of the Arithmetic Reader, many compositions made by the children, and supplementary reading matter, representing and applying what the children learn and do in the various studies and exercises of the grade are to be read.

Spelling:

See what is said on this subject in first year work. Never accept any misspelled manuscript.

THIRD YEAR.

Seeing, Talking and Writing:

Continue the making of compositions, oral and written, *i. e.*, the making of descriptions, narrations and comparisons. Subjects may be taken from plant lessons, animal lessons, human body lessons, vapor lessons or other geography lessons, etc., etc.

Many imaginary stories should be written based on the knowledge the children have gained of the growth and habits of plants and animals and of evaporation and the various forms of condensed vapor.

The children should be trained to reproduce short descriptions, narrations and comparisons. The compositions for reproduction should in no case be taken from books to which the children have access. The compositions reproduced should give the entire thought of the selection in its proper order. It is by no means desirable to have the children reproduce the words of the selections read to them.

Some attention should be given to writing letters. Teach with care how to begin and how to close an ordinary letter, and how to direct the envelope.

Spelling:

Do not accept a manuscript with a misspelled word in it.

Reading:

Two Third Readers, the Arithmetic Reader, sixty pages of the Health Primer, and much written matter made by the children may be read.

Composition and Grammatic Idiom:

The children are expected to learn by observation and directed effort how to put the English sentence on the written page.

They must know therefore :
1. How to begin the first word of each sentence.
2. How to close each kind of sentence. (They must know therefore each kind of sentence—Declarative, Interrogative, Exclaiming, Commanding.)
3. How to write proper names. (They must distinguish therefore between a common name and a particular name.)
4. How to write *I* and *O* as words.
5. How to write the possessive forms of nouns. Special work will be required here.
6. How to write such abbreviations as they use, especially those beginning with capital letters and closing with periods.
7. How to spell the plural forms of all nouns they use. They should know these as plural forms, and should know also the corresponding singular forms as such.
8. How to use quotation marks in writing ordinary narration.
9. How to divide words at the end of a line, and how to use the hyphen in a few compound words.

They should know also :
1. How to use the present, past and complete forms of the irregular verbs enumerated in first grade work, and of a few other verbs which the teacher may find desirable to give. The child should know which form of each of these verbs should be used with *have, has* and *had.* The children must be able to tabulate these three forms of the verbs. When given either of the three forms of any verb they have learned, they should be able to give the other two promptly.
2. How to use the comparative forms of adverbs and adjectives. These are taught most easily and most effectively by much object work.

FOURTH YEAR.

Composition—Oral and Written:

The subjects for composition may be taken from the physical geography lessons and the physiology lessons, but to avoid monotony these may be interspersed with descriptions of pictures, plants and animals, which may also be made to contribute to a better knowledge of geography, or when possible to a better knowledge of the work in physiology and hygiene. Much care will be necessary to preserve unity in composition, for in some cases many lessons will be required for the development of a single subject, as, "Bones" or "Digestion." In every case it is desirable, when finishing a subject, to cause the pupil to make for himself a list of topics representing the parts of the subject to be followed in talking or writing. In this way unity and method will be taught the child. The teacher must not forget that the purpose of all this work, as language work, is to train the child to see subjects as entireties, and to give him power in the use of his vocabulary, to represent in idiomatic English, connectedly and methodically, subjects as entireties (units of associate thought in connected discourse). To do this properly the child must receive much help from the teacher in the use of composition idiom.

Letter-writing should be continued to include much variety in forms of friendly letters and answers.

The children should have some practice in writing imaginary stories based on their knowledge of the facts of nature, especially those relating to physical geography ; as, The History of a Grain of Sand ; The Story of the Spring, etc., etc.

The children should also write some reproductions in each kind of composition, description, narration and comparison.

The children should learn to separate the English sentence into subject and predicate. See "Fifth Grade Manual" on this subject.

Grammatic Idiom:

Train the children to use correctly at least fifty of the most common irregular verbs of the language. Cause them to know which form of the verb is used to represent absolute past time, and which form is used with *have*, *has* and *had*. To teach the common irregular verbs more efficiently, teach in comparison *sit* with *set*, *lie* with *lay*, *teach* with *learn*, *rise* with *raise*. In teaching these last named verbs, let the pupils frequently give the meanings of words in their different forms as they use them, as ; "I lay the book on the table" means "I place the book on the table ; " "The dog lay on the rug" means "The dog rested or reclined on the rug," etc., etc. The children must learn to see meanings in forms, and accordingly must be practiced in using forms. In teaching the irregular verbs, care must be taken with the different uses of the present participles. Children should be trained to use this form of the verb for economy in the use of words, and for elegance of expression.

Spelling :

The words used in all written matter must be correctly spelled. If the child be trained, and by this time he should be, to feel and to understand that he must know how to spell a word before trying to write it, and to take a pride in correctly-spelled manuscript, the subject of spelling will be greatly simplified. For reviews and test exercises from time to time to impress unusual orthography and to fasten the spelling of words, not frequently used in the child's written work, the teacher may select suitable words from the reading and geography lessons. These selected words should be assigned the pupils as tasks in learning to spell.

Much hard work will be required to secure good spelling.

Reading:

Two Fourth Readers, Scribner's Geographical Reader, and other reading matter to supplement the work in geography ; also, matter to supplement, explain, and interest the child in the work in physiology may be read.

Read no supplementary matter, except for the definite purpose of explaining or expanding the geography work or the science work of the grade. In doing this supplementary reading, the children must be trained to get thought from the printed page. This requires especial care on the part of the teacher, as the child must be taught to work economically as well as intelligently. Hitherto, the printed page has been to the child in the main the representation in words of that which he already knew ; hereafter the printed page must be to him in the main a source of information. This is a new use of the book which the child now can learn neither too soon nor too well. Until he has learned this use of the book, he has not learned to read, no matter how well he may pronounce aloud the words and sentences found therein.

The Normal Fourth Reader is to be read only as far as page 209.

FIFTH YEAR.

Composition—Oral and Written:

Continue the work of description, narration and comparison. Let much work be done in reproducing with accuracy and rapidity, descriptions, stories and comparisons read to the children.

In addition to these reproductions, the teacher may take other subjects, as tableaux, pictures, subjects from the pupils' lessons in geography or science, and train the pupils to make outlines, or name the parts that make the wholes, till the pupils have acquired some degree of strength in separating subjects into parts. Then pupils should be trained to make short compositions, following the outlines made.

Accuracy, both of construction and of expression, composition characterized by completeness and method, as well as by correct verbal expression, is the product at first to be sought in this grade. The compositions should, therefore, be short. Work for exact representation and correct diction as the result of the first effort, so that the habit of talking or writing carelessly at first, if it has been acquired, may be corrected. Note-book work is sometimes bad because of this pernicious habit.

In all this work help the child to the composition idiom that his vocabulary lacks.

Letter forms should be given, and should include the conventional forms of invitations and responses.

Composition and Grammatic Idiom:

The simple sentence may be considered; the subject and predicate taught; the base or foundation of each discovered; the influence of added words on the base of the subject; on the base of the predicate; to what other word each word in the sentence relates; its influence on that word.

The parts of speech may be taught; the forms of personal

pronouns and their uses in the simple sentence; the forms of relative pronouns, and their uses in the simplest form of complex sentences; the three forms of adjectives and adverbs, and their uses in the simple sentence.

There should be frequent practice in the use of irregular verbs. (See syllabus of language work for this grade.)

Reading:

The Normal Fourth Reader from page 209, completed. The Franklin Intermediate Reader.

Much supplementary matter should be used, but in all cases it should be such as will lead to a better understanding and a broader view of the geography, history and physiology work of the grade. The supplementary reading should be done in all cases for a specific purpose. The children should be taught how to read for this purpose. (See what is said on this subject in Fourth Grade work.)

Spelling:

In addition to the correct spelling of all words used in written work, the teacher may make a selection of words not frequently used, and other words whose spelling requires special attention from Merrill's Word and Sentence Book to page 65.

SIXTH YEAR.

Composition—Oral and Written:

Continue the work of making oral and written compositions—descriptions, narrations and comparisons. Let the subjects be taken from the geography work, the physiology and the history work of the grade. In every case cause an outline of the subject to be made before the pupils talk or write, and see that in talking or writing they follow the outline. Lead pupils to give the selected parts of the subject their proportional values; that is, lead them to appreciate the value of making their compositions symmetrical.

To give variety to the exercises from time to time the pupils may write reproductions or descriptions of pictures.

Letter-writing should be continued, including formal letters of inquiry and application and replies.

The analysis of sentences must be continued. Sentences involving all the uses of subordinate clauses are to be a specialty of the grade. The uses of clauses are nearly identical with those of nouns.

Grammatic Idiom :

Let the pupils learn the different kinds of nouns, the different forms that nouns assume, and the different uses of nouns in the simple sentence. Complete an outline like the following :

Nouns.
- Kinds
  - common
  - proper
    - ordinary.
    - verbal.
    - abstract.
- Forms
  - singular
    - ordinary.
    - possessive.
  - plural
    - ordinary.
    - possessive.
- Uses
  - subject.
  - object of verb.
  - object of preposition—better, called the idea part of a phrase of which the preposition is the relation part.
  - complement or attribute (adjective).
  - adjective (appositive).
  - adjective without change of form.
  - adjective by change of form.
  - adjective (possessive form).
  - adverb.

Study pronouns, adjectives and verbs in a similar way.

The pupil should be able to make an outline for each of the above-named parts of speech, corresponding to that given for the noun, and when called on to do so should be able to explain any part of such outline giving two or more illustrations.

Reading:

The New Fifth Reader. Supplementary reading matter should in all cases be such as will contribute to a broader view of the geography work and the history work of this grade.

Read to know more of people, their customs and habits of life; of cities and their distinguishing characteristics; of sections of countries and their products. Read always with maps before the children, and make constant reference to these maps.

Read "The Courtship of Miles Standish" and "Evangeline" in connection with the history work of the grade.

Read to know more of historical characters, of people represented by historical characters, of people and places referred to in the history work of the grade.

Poems and anecdotes having relation to the history or to the geography work of the grade may be read aloud with much profit, and extracts, "gems," selected from the same may be preserved in writing by the pupils for future use.

Spelling:

As in the work of previous grades, the difficult words of the various lessons should be selected by the teacher and assigned the pupils as special work in spelling. Especial work on difficult words so concenters the efforts of the learner on spelling in general as to make of him a good speller. Use also Merrill's Word and Sentence Book to page 125.

SEVENTH YEAR.

Composition—Oral and Written:

The composition of this grade should consist chiefly of paragraphing to be applied to all the work of the grade. Train the children to grasp a principle that may be expressed by a definition or a rule and then lead them to express the principle, that is to give a well worded concise statement of the entire thought in mind; as, "the rate of profit is expressed by the quotient obtained by dividing the profit by one per cent. of the cost."

Much good paragraphing may be done in the technical language work; as "a sentence having one or more subordinate clauses is called a complex sentence." The teacher must not accept definitions that have been learned as products in paragraphing.

The work in physics offers especially good opportunity for skillful paragraphing.

Geography and history offer the most prolific and at the same time the most profitable field for exercises in paragraph making. At the beginning of the year the paragraphs will be short, necessarily, consisting sometimes of a single simple or complex or compound sentence. The children, however, will grow stronger in seeing larger entireties and in distinguishing the main from the dependent facts of a group of related ideas and will learn to put them together as a paragraph.

In writing paragraphs for making more formal compositions, especial care must be given to teach structure, a proper sequence and a pleasing symmetry.

For variety, poetry may be transformed to prose. A careful selection of poems to be transformed will be required, as few poems are fitted for this work. Be careful to secure a faithful reproduction of the thought, adding nothing to and omitting nothing of the thought of the poem transformed. Let the poem be transformed as faithfully as a paragraph of Latin should be translated, remembering that the work is done for the cultivation of ability to express faithfully and elegantly the exact thought of the author. At first pupils will require much help from the teacher. This work will require much attention to the choice of words, as well as to the choice of idioms.

Letter-writing should be continued, including letters of congratulation and of regret and sympathy, also various forms of business letters.

Analysis of sentences must be continued. The work should involve a well expressed analysis of any prose sentence that may be placed before the child.

Grammatic Idiom:

Study all the parts of speech, making an outline for each, omitting sources.

See outline of the noun in the sixth grade work. Study also the following outline:

Verbs.
- Kinds
  - according to use: transitive, intransitive.
  - according to form: regular, irregular.
- Forms
  - infinitive.
  - present: ordinary, third person singular.
  - present participle.
  - past participle.
- Use
  - predicate base: finite, infinitive.
  - as noun { Give all uses as noun.
  - as adjective.
  - as adverb.

Give special drill
 (a) In the use of collective nouns;
 (b) In the use of nouns having plural forms only;
 (c) In the use of nouns having the same form for both singular and plural;
 (d) In the use of personal pronouns,
  1st, In compound subjects;
  2d, In compound predicate-nominatives;
  3d, In compound objects, both after verbs and after prepositions.

Teach the uses of the comma in a succession of particulars, and with an appositive; also the most common use of the semicolon.

Use Kerl's Language Lessons.

Reading:

Normal Fifth Reader.

Select supplementary reading matter to explain and broaden the work in history especially. Some of this, as poems and short descriptions, may be read aloud, from which representative passages, "gems," may be selected by the pupil to be preserved for future use. The pupil should in all cases select for himself such representative passages after a careful reading of the poem or article in which the passages are found.

Spelling:

All written work should be absolutely correct in this particular. For emphasis on important selected words, Merrill's Word and Sentence Book may be used.

EIGHTH YEAR.

Composition—Oral and Written:

The subjects for composition should be taken chiefly from the work of the grade, physiology affording excellent themes for description, and history affording excellent themes for narration, and especially for comparison and contrast.

The pupils should be exercised in making brief but well worded and connected abstracts of chapters or articles read in the supplementary work of history and physical geography. The children should be expected to show how well they have heard and understood by expressing themselves, in short, well-arranged, well-worded paragraphs.

Cultivate the ability to make a brief abstract correct at first writing after once reading or once hearing a short article.

The pupils of this grade should be led to see that composition is embraced under two heads, structure and style, and that the more important of these is structure. They should be made to see the importance of selection (a topical view); of method (a proper order of the selected topics); of symmetry (a proper emphasis of the selected topics); of unity (a proper continuity of purpose in the effort of speaking or writing).

Invention:

Transform the poem "Lilly's Ball," making good prose of it,

neither omitting anything of nor adding anything to the thought of the poem.

Invent at least three other prose stories, with birds, insects, the smaller mammals, vegetables, forest trees, gems or the individuals of some other group of natural objects as actors.

Pupils should be taught the use of the simile, the metaphor, the comparison; the use of quotation for embellishment and emphasis; the use of description for the embellishment of narration, and the use of climax, or sequential order, in the presentation of particulars.

1. Make in simple narration of facts a story based on a series of pictures, setting forth the facts. This first draft of the composition will be short, naturally.
2. Rewrite this story, introducing brief descriptions of persons and other important objects.
3. Rewrite it, introducing appropriate "simile." The pupils must work to get similes that are appropriate.
4. Rewrite it, introducing metaphor, retaining the simile as far as may be done.
5. Rewrite it, introducing quotations for embellishment or explanation or for both.
6. Rewrite it, making an introduction and a conclusion.

The style of speaking and writing will be improved by a proper study of the composition and grammatic idiom hereafter enumerated.

The pupils must be able to analyze any sentence in prose or verse that may be placed before them.

Composition and Grammatic Idiom:

Study
1. All the uses of the present participle. Give practice in the use of the present participle in abridging incorrect compound sentences.
2. All the uses of the perfect participle. Give the pupils practice in the use of the perfect participle for abridgment.
3. All the uses of the infinitive.
4. All the uses of the subordinate clause.

5. Each part of speech according to the following outline:

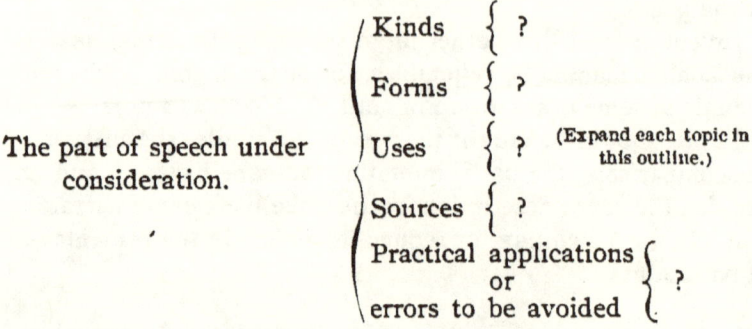

The part of speech under consideration.
{ Kinds { ?
  Forms { ?
  Uses { ? (Expand each topic in this outline.)
  Sources { ?
  Practical applications or errors to be avoided } ? }

See outline of the nouns in the sixth grade work. See also the following outline of sources of nouns:

Sources { Original.
  Derived from { connectives.
    verbs.
    adjectives.
    other nouns. }

In the study of sources under each part of speech, the Word Analysis prescribed for the grade may be used. This work need not include more than twenty roots from each of which many of our words are derived, but should be thorough in giving the common suffixes and prefixes.

Teach the uses of the colon, the semicolon, and the comma as found in ordinary composition.

Reading:

The reading of Whittier's "Snow Bound" and of Irving's "Legend of Sleepy Hollow" is prescribed for the grade work.

The reading necessary for the development of the work in history and physical geography will constitute the rest of the work in this branch. This includes works of fiction. Some of this, as spirited narratives, interesting descriptions in prose or verse, should be read aloud, from which representative or beautiful passages should be selected and preserved for embellishment and explanation in compositions to be written through the year.

Number.

FIRST YEAR.
(See Teachers' Manual in pamphlet form.)

SECOND YEAR.
(See Teachers' Manual in pamphlet form.)

THIRD YEAR.
(See Teachers' Manual in pamphlet form.)

FOURTH YEAR.

Continue the work of addition, multiplication, subtraction and division, using denominate numbers and abstract numbers. Use such simple and compound denominate numbers as relate to ordinary domestic and business life. Use only small abstract numbers, but train the children to work accurately and rapidly with them.

Pupils should be expected to add small numbers involving those fractions only whose terms are small numbers, that is, fractions whose common denominators can be seen readily.

In subtraction, fractions may be used in the subtrahend or in the minuend, never in both.

In multiplication, fractions may be used in the multiplicand or in the multiplier, never in both.

Abstract fractions should be used sparingly in this grade; the pupils should be made to consider fractional parts of things chiefly, things with which they are familiar.

Pupils should be exercised in getting parts of large numbers involving fractions in the results and in partial results. Problems should be given involving fractions in their partial results, the fraction in every case being easily understood.

Whole numbers applied to things may be measured by fractional parts of like things.

Tenths and hundredths expressed decimally should be used first in addition and subtraction, then as multiplicands and dividends with whole numbers for multipliers and divisors. After this work tenths may be employed as multipliers and divisors of whole numbers.

Much work should be given involving the use of the table of dollars and cents.

Pupils should be expected to do accurate work at all times. After learning to do accurate work, they may be trained to work rapidly.

Mental exercises should constitute a part of every recitation, in which children should be required frequently to make their own problems and to solve the same in the hearing of the class. The language of the pupil should be carefully guarded and corrected in all this work.

Multipliers need never exceed numbers occupying three places; divisors need not exceed numbers occupying two places.

The time of the recitation should be given chiefly to the development of principles, and to ascertaining their applications. Class practice should be restricted to the use of small numbers that the learner may give his whole attention to mastering principles and their practical applications, and to acquiring the ability to see quickly the relations of numbers in problematic statements.

It is best to restrict the recitation time given to the solution of problems that can be solved without the use of the pencil. These should be varied that the minds of the children may be kept active. They should be made more and more complicated that the children may learn to see relations of quantities and numbers that are very much involved. Such work should prepare the pupils to do the examples found in the book as seat work. Practice with large numbers should be expected of the pupils as seat work. This latter practice must not be neglected in which the pupil must be held accountable for correct results.

For practice exercises the pupils may use the Elementary Arithmetic.

The ability of the pupils to solve the problems of the book

without help, is the measure of the efficiency of the class or recitation work. The children should receive no help in their efforts to understand the problems assigned them for seat work.

The Intellectual Arithmetic may be used by the pupils. This book should be in the hands of pupils only during the time of recitation. The book should be closed frequently by all the pupils except the one who is asked to read the problem to be solved. At other times the pupils may read problems and solve them, as they are called upon miscellaneously by the teacher. This is not a book to be studied.

FIFTH YEAR.

The pupils of this grade are expected to master fractions, common and decimal. At first consider only fractions of things, and for *four months*, at least, use those fractions only whose terms are small numbers, that is, use those fractions only whose common unit the children can see or determine by inspection.

The work from the beginning should involve the solution of problems.

If small whole numbers be multiplied by fractions until the pupils see that to multiply by a fraction is to take a part of a number, the multiplication of a fraction by a fraction may be easily understood, and children will appreciate that multiplying by a fraction is, in fact, dividing or taking one or more parts.

If small whole numbers be measured by fractions, children may be led to measure fractions by fractions, and will appreciate that dividing by a fraction is measuring and not separating.

During the progress of this preliminary work the pupils will do better work without books. It is desirable to give variety to the work of every recitation. Variety does not confuse the pupil who understands the reason for what he does.

Later in the year numbers may be factored; common denominators may be obtained by means of factors, and operations with more difficult fractions may be made.

The Elementary Arithmetic may be used for seat work and test exercises.

Exercises supplementing this work may be taken from the

Intellectual Arithmetic. For the use of this book, see directions given in the fourth grade.

The relation between decimal and common fractions should be made clear to the pupils by changing one to the other, using such fractions only as can be changed without use of slate and pencil.

Children should be able to see the sum of ½, .5, and ⅓, or .75, ¼, and ⅓, as readily as they will see the sum of ½, ½, and ⅓, or ¾ and ¼ and ⅓.

The time of the recitation should be given chiefly to the development of principles, and to ascertaining their applications. Class practice should be restricted to the use of small numbers that the learner may give his whole attention to mastering principles and their practical applications. Practice with large numbers should be expected of the pupils as seat work. This latter practice must not be neglected in which the pupil must be held accountable for correct results.

It is best to restrict the recitation time given to the solution of problems that can be solved without the use of the pencil. These should be varied that the minds of the children may be kept active. They should be made more and more complicated that the children may learn to see relations of quantities and numbers that are very much involved. Such work should prepare the pupils to do the examples found in the book as seat work. The ability of the pupils to solve the problems of the book without help, is the measure of the efficiency of the class or recitation work. The children should receive no help in their efforts to understand the problems assigned them for seat work.

SIXTH YEAR.

The work of this year is chiefly with compound denominate numbers. The work will be simplified and lightened by using numbers applied to things that the pupils thoroughly understand and know about, and, when possible, things that can be seen and weighed or measured in the school-room, and by using small numbers, particularly the first half of the year.

In the application of the above remark the teacher will find it desirable to ignore many denominations, as; gills, drachms, quarters, hundredweight, and some entire tables, as cloth measure, etc. It is not desirable to teach pupils of this grade the metric system of weights and measures.

Pupils should be made intelligent by the study of relations and by computations made after actual measurement, particularly in long measure, square measure, cubic measure and board measure. Pupils will be aided in seeing relations by giving them examples involving purchasing in higher denominations and selling in lower denominations and fractional parts thereof; examples in buying fractional parts of higher denominations and selling in lower denominations and fractional parts thereof; examples calling for actual measurement, as carpeting, papering, fencing, paving, and the like, involving the application of a definite unit of measurement.

It is not desirable to teach exhaustively one table and the work belonging to it before going to another. It is not wise for instance to postpone the teaching of cubic measure to the last of the year or until all other subjects have been thoroughly mastered.

Pupils must see that matter (things) about which they learn occupies space and has weight, must see the necessity for standards of measurement, and must be made to understand the unit by which the value (amount) of each quality of the object is determined.

Pupils should be practiced in estimating values of all kinds by comparison with other values of like kind, and then with the standard unit of measurement or estimation. This will cultivate judgment and lead to the exercise of care in deciding.

Pupils must be able to show by diagram, in cases where it is possible to do it, the number of standard units contained in specified distances, surfaces and volumes. This amount of representation is necessary to show a full and correct understanding of the subject (this applies in an especial manner to the measuring of lumber and timber, of wood and of stone).

In doing the practical work in the application of denominate numbers excellent opportunity is given for the best possible review of fractions. The child who forgets fractions while learning denominate numbers is not working to the best advantage.

Pupils are aided in their grasp of denominate numbers by doing much work in seeing the relation of one quantity to another expressed in different denominations of the same table, and then in expressing such relation fractionally. For instance, What part of a gallon is one-half of a pint? What part of a bushel and a half are two and a half quarts? How many times will a block two inches wide, four inches long and three inches high, contain the half of an inch cube? How many times will it contain a half inch cube? etc., etc.

The time of the recitation should be given chiefly to the development of principles, and to ascertaining their applications. Class practice should be restricted to the use of small numbers that the learner may give his whole attention to mastering principles and their practical applications.

It is best to restrict the recitation time to the solution of problems that can be solved without the use of the pencil. These should be varied that the minds of the children may be kept active. They should be made more and more complicated that the children may learn to see relations of quantities and numbers that are very much involved. Such work should prepare the pupils to do the examples found in the book as seat work.

Practice with large numbers should be expected of the pupils as seat work. This latter practice must not be neglected in which the pupils must be held accountable for correct results.

The ability of the pupils to solve the problems of the book without help, is the measure of the efficiency of the class or recitation work. The children should receive no help in their efforts to understand the problems assigned them for seat work.

Pupils are expected to be able to get the areas of triangles whose heights and bases are known, and of parallelograms whose heights and bases are known and to prove the same by geometry.

They should be taught to estimate the surfaces of cubes and how to get areas of circles, and should be expected to get areas of the convex surfaces of cones and of prisms.

The National Arithmetic may be used for seat work and test examples.

Exercises supplementing this work may be taken from the Intellectual Arithmetic. For the use of this book, see directions given in the fourth year work.

SEVENTH YEAR.

Percentage and its applications. The National Arithmetic to be used by the pupils.

Exercises supplementing this work may be taken from the Intellectual Arithmetic. For the use of this book, see directions given in the fourth year work.

Make an outline of percentage, showing the relations of the applications of percentage to Percentage proper.

TABULAR VIEW.

Percentage	base	rate.	percentage.	amount	
Profit and Loss.	buying price	rate.	profit or loss	selling price	
Commission.	amount of transactions	rate.	commission.		
	proceeds	rate.	commission.	amount of transactions	
Taxes	valuation	rate.	tax		
Duties	value	rate.	duty	new value	
Interest	principle	rate.	interest	amount	time
Insurance	amount insured	rate.	premium		time

Let pupils be trained to give concise statements involving both definitions and directions for obtaining; as, "the rate of commission is the quotient of the commission by the commission at one per cent.," etc. Distinguish between a statement and a rule. Pupils should be able to give both, but should not be allowed to give one when asked to give the other.

Teach Ratio and Simple Proportion. Avoid complex work. Let pupils be able to analyze any example which they may solve by proportion, noting the philosophy and value of the shorter way of working involving cancellation.

In the application of percentage to the business of life excellent opportunity is offered for a practical and profitable review of fractions and of denominate numbers. The child who in learning percentage, has lost his knowledge of fractions and denominate numbers, has largely failed in his work. Much good work may be done by applying percentage to fractional numbers; as, what per cent. of $4\frac{1}{2}$ is $\frac{1}{3}$? etc., etc. In a corresponding way, good work may be done by applying percentage to denominate numbers.

The time of the recitation should be given chiefly to the development of principles, and to ascertaining their applications. Class practice should be restricted to the use of small numbers that the learner may give his whole attention to mastering principles and their practical applications.

It is best to restrict the recitation time to the solution of problems that can be solved without the use of the pencil. These should be varied that the minds of the children may be kept active. They should be made more and more complicated that the children may learn to see relations of quantities and numbers that are very much involved. Such work should prepare the pupils to do the examples found in the book as seat work.

Practice with large numbers should be expected of the pupils as seat work. This latter practice must not be neglected in which the pupils must be held accountable for correct results.

The ability of the pupils to solve the problems of the book without help, is the measure of the efficiency of the class or recitation work. The children should receive no help in their efforts to understand the problems assigned them for seat work.

EIGHTH YEAR.

1. Review the entire subject of numbers. By this review the pupils should be made to see the fundamental principles underlying all operations in numbers. While doing this work, a systematic training in mental arithmetic should be given. This may be had by using the Intellectual Arithmetic. This book should be in the hands of the pupils only at the time of recitation.

2. A careful review of the business applications of percentage should be given. The ordinary business forms should be taught, including business letters. Difficult puzzling examples should be avoided.

3. Study powers and roots.

4. Study mensuration.

The work found in the book on the subject of mensuration should be made objective wherever it is possible to do so. The teacher is asked to consult an elementary geometry before beginning this work; care must be taken to give pupils correct ideas of what they try to learn. Inventional Geometry, by Wm. George Spencer, is furnished the teacher as a companion book while giving this work.

5. Let the pupils solve by analysis all the examples on pages 305 and 306 before attempting to state them by proportion.

6. Let pupils perform the test examples found on pages 329 and 338 in the school-room without help, but not in time of recitation. The time of recitation can be used much more profitable than in solving and explaining difficult problems.

ALGEBRA.

Wentworth's Elements of Algebra through chapter VIII, omitting case II, page 118.

Suggestion: It is believed that the teacher will find it profitable to give a general idea of an equation and its use, having the pupils learn the axioms involved in making changes in the equation, and having them solve many of the problems beginning on page 69 of Wentworth; also those found in the early pages of Davies's and Sensenig's Algebras before taking up the work of Wentworth by course. The teacher is advised also to examine Sensenig's Algebra (to be found on his desk) for suggestions respecting other elementary and preparatory work before taking up Wentworth by course.

NOTE.—The Rules provide that two years may be allowed for completing the studies of this Grade, each class is to be divided into two sections —First Section and Second Section—the less advanced to be designated the First Section and the more advanced the Second Section.

Geography.

THIRD YEAR.

A. Physical Geography.

(For explanations of suggestion and experiments, see Appendix to this work.)

I.

Air :

1. Some of its properties :
    (a) It is tasteless ;
    (b) It can not be seen ;
    (c) It is transparent ;
    (d) It can be felt ;
    (e) When heated, it rises.

II.

Vapor :

1. Evaporation and condensation :
    (a) Give many illustrations of the "drying" that is constantly going on from every moist surface ;
    (b) Show that heat changes water into vapor ;
    (c) Show that the coolness of the air changes its vapor to water-dust ;
    (d) Show that warm air changes water-dust into vapor;
    (e) Show that the air is full of moisture.

2. Sources of vapor :
    (a) Water changed to vapor by artificial heat ;
    (b) Water changed to vapor by the heat of the sun ; from brooks, rivers, lakes, etc.; from streets, grass, trees, etc.; from every wet surface.

3. Different forms of vapor:
    (a) Dew: Show
        (1) That vapor in air is changed to water by chilling the air;
        (2) That cold grass, leaves, etc., at night, chill the air near them, changing its vapor into water-dust;
        (3) That dew is more noticeable on certain nights than on others.
    (b) Frost:
        The frozen dew on grass, leaves, etc.
    (c) Clouds: Show
        (1) That the air is full of vapor;
        (2) That contact with cold air changes the vapor to water-dust that floats in the air in different and changing forms.
    (d) Rain:
        Show that by the uniting of the floating drops of water or water-dust, larger drops, too heavy to float, are formed.
    (e) Hail:
        Frozen rain.
    (f) Snow:
        Frozen water-dust.
    (g) Sleet:
        Snow-flakes partly melted by warm wind.
    (h) Fog, Mist, etc.:
        Changes of weather noted each day; changes in length of days noted; changes in length of shadows; direction of wind, etc., etc.

B. Map Making and Reading:

1. Develop the idea of *relative size*; train pupils to estimate distances; train them in the use of common terms of measurement.
2. Develop, by means of objects, ideas of
    (a) *Relative position.* Use terms *up, down; right, left; back, front,* etc.
    (b) *Absolute direction.* Use the term *east, west, north, south.* Teach cardinal points. Show the compass.

3. Maps:
   (a) Draw maps of the teacher's desk or of the pupil's desk in varying *scales*, giving much practice in representing the relative positions of objects. Let the pictures at first be drawn on paper or on slates and placed on the floor or desks, with north lines towards the north, etc. Then hang on wall, north at the top, on the north side of the room; afterwards on the other sides.
   (b) Draw maps of the school-room with objects located; of the school-room with added halls, etc.
   (c) Draw plan of school building with added yard, etc.; of the school building with street and adjoining buildings.
   (d) Draw maps representing all additions to the maps already drawn; to represent all parts of the city studied; any portion of the country visited and studied; to represent what is seen in pictures or in relief or sand maps.
   (e) During the course, pupils should be led to devise ways of representing on maps, railway lines, steam, horse, electric; rivers, bridges, small streams, canals, boundaries; in fact, all facts usually found on city maps.
   (f) Give much practice in *Reading Maps*.

C. **Places to be Studied:**
1. School Building:
   Material used in building; sources of material—how made; people who made it; its purpose; location; government; by whom owned.
2. Block in which school building is situated:
   (a) Surroundings, trees, lamps, streets, pavements, letter boxes, parking, etc.
   (b) Bounding of the block; direction of streets and the slope.
   (c) Maps in sand and on paper, showing as many of the discovered facts as possible.

3. Adjacent blocks—Neighborhood:
    Study a sufficient number of blocks to show the plan of the city.
    (a) Location and names of important buildings, parks, circles, statues, streets, car lines.
    (b) Let the map-making keep pace with the observation lessons. Give much practice in showing *relative position* of places and *direction* of places.
4. Other parts of the city to be studied:
    White House.   Treasury Department.
    State Department.   Bureau of Engraving and
    Pension Office.   Printing.
    Patent Office.   Agricultural Department.
    Smithsonian.   Monument.
    Navy Yard.   Museum.
                      Capitol.
    (a) Study the places with reference to *locations*, and *relative positions*.
    (b) Briefly study what is done in these buildings, and learn a few important facts about them. Use many pictures in this work. Use the map constantly.
5. The city as a whole:
    (a) Its location—advantages.
    (b) Plan of the city—four divisions; the Capitol the geographical center; the business center.
    (c) In this work, do much map reading. Discover horse-car lines, steam railroad lines, depots, schools, parks, well-known hotels, business houses, etc.
    (d) History—for whom named, etc.
6. A section outside of the city (to be visited by the children):
    (a) Study physical features—hill, valley, ravine, plain, creek, river. Observe the action of water with reference to the drainage of the section studied. Apply to drainage of larger sections.
    (b) Mold in sand and draw on paper, discovering ways of representing facts observed.

7. Places near the city and bounding the city (to be visited by the children):
    (a) Rock creek.
    (b) Potomac river:
        (1) Bridges.
        (2) Landings—wharf.
        (3) Kinds of business on water front.
        (4) Whence comes its water?
        (5) In what direction is its flowing?
    (c) Arlington, Soldiers' Home, Meridian Hill, Suburban Towns. Use maps and pictures. Read maps of the District of Columbia.

D. **How People Live:**

   (a) Buildings—Dwellings:

   Home life under different conditions, such as nationality, classes. Home interiors, schools, churches.

   Stores—Kinds:

   Such as dry goods, clothing, hardware, furniture, grocery, provision, fuel, markets.

   Where articles are procured—source, how brought to the city, how delivered to consumers, etc.

   Why are stores grouped centrally?

   (b) Occupations of the people:

   (1) Means of transportation:

   People: Cars—horse, electric, cable, carriages, cabs, etc.

   Merchandise: Wagons, cars, boats, etc.

   (2) Means of communication:

   Messengers.

   Letters:—Study postal system—letter boxes, carriers, post offices, stamps, etc.

   Telephone—Telegraph:

   Wires, poles, central offices.

(3) Means of lighting houses and city :
   Lamps.
   Gas—system of pipes under city—where made, etc.
   Electric lamps—wire, power house.
(4) Water of the city :
   Trace its course from river to house.
   Pumps, hydrants, fire plugs, etc.
(5) How the city is protected :
   Fire department.
   Police department.
(6) Government.
   Home, school, city.

E. Teach by use of the map of the United States, the locations of a few important cities proceeding from the District of Columbia by imaginary journeys, by both rail and water, to adjoining States causing the children to trace such journeys on the map. These cities should be compared with Washington in their general characteristics.

The relative positions of these cities should be studied, as well as their relative distances from Washington, and from one another.

SUGGESTIONS TO TEACHERS.

1. Always bear in mind the purpose of this unit of work ; it is :
   (1) That the pupil may see and read geographical facts as represented on maps ;
   (2) That he may know by actual observation a certain definite portion of the earth's surface.
   (3) That he may know by actual observation something of the life of the people living within this section.
   (4) That, by means of these known standards, all subsequent study of unknown parts of the earth and of unknown people may be, by comparison, understood.

Cautions.

2. Avoid unnecessary detail in the study of places.
3. Aim to make the children see in maps *real* pictures of places.

APPENDIX.

EXPERIMENTS IN PHYSICAL GEOGRAPHY.

I.

Air:

1. Properties:

    For (a), (b), (c), (d), no experiments need be suggested.

    (e) When heated, air rises:

    (1) Hold the hand over lamp, over register, over candle, over radiator, etc., etc.

    (2) Hold piece of smoking paper in fire-place. Use the smoking paper in (1). Current of air may be seen carrying the smoke.

    (3) Hang threads, pieces of paper or spiral cut from paper, over lamp, register, candle, etc. Currents of air move them.

2. Air in motion:

    (a) Draughts:

    (1) Place lamp chimney at the edge of table over a short candle. Hold smoking paper at the side of lower opening. Direction of currents—draught—shown by smoke.

    (2) Hold burning candle at cracks of doors and windows; at fire-places, ventilating shafts, etc.

II

Vapor in the Air:

1. Evaporation and condensation:

    (a) (1) Moisten slates with damp sponge; observe the disappearance of water.

(2) Observe water in shallow dishes in the schoolroom; in tumblers, marking the decrease day by day.
(3) Observe drying of pavements after rain.
(4) Observe drying of clothes hung on lines.
(5) Dip the hand in water and wave in the air.
(6) Pour a few drops of alcohol on slate; observe its rapid disappearance.
(7) Heat water over a flame; it disappears.

(b) Heat changes water into vapor:
    (2) Tea-kettle and oil stove. By constant boiling water *disappears*.

(c) (1) Hold a plate or tumbler in the cloud of steam; it will be covered with fine drops, showing that the water of the kettle has gone from the kettle into the air;
(2) Hold a cold, dry plate close to the mouth of the spout where *nothing can be seen*. The plate becomes covered with drops of water, showing that this clear space was filled with water that could not be seen—vapor.

(d) (4) Hold a candle under the cloud of visible steam issuing from the spout. It disappears—is changed by the heat to vapor.

2. Sources of vapor:
(a) Artificial Heat:
    (1) Heating of liquids on stoves and with gas; drying of clothes before fires, etc.

(b) All parts of the earth heated by the sun. Air coming in contact with heated portions is heated and rises. The surfaces of bodies of water or bodies that are wet or moist are heated; the water is gradually changed to vapor, which is carried in the rising air in all directions and to great heights. Use experiments given to illustrate this.

3. Different forms in which this vapor is seen:
   (a) Dew:
       (1) Carry a dry pitcher into school room. Fill it with ice water. Observe the drops forming on the outside. Vapor in air changed to water.
       (2) Breathe on window glass or mirror. Dimness due to condensation of moisture in breath.
       (3) At night grass, trees, walks, etc., become cool, owing to the absence of sun-heat. The air coming in contact with them is chilled and the vapor is changed to water, as on the pitcher.
       (4) Variation of amount of dew, due to variation in the amount of moisture in the air and in the coldness of objects.
   (b) Frost—Frozen Dew:
       Why is it on the *inside* of windows? Observe the change from frost to dew and from dew to vapor, under the influence of sun-heat. Study this on a frosty morning.
   (c) Clouds:
       Use experiments described under vapor, tea-kettle and stove, etc.
       Observe the appearance of a cloud in a clear sky, and its sudden disappearance; also changes in form. Lead to explanation.
   (d) Rain:
       In holding the plate in the cloud of steam, observe how the water-dust gathers into drops that roll down the plate.
       Hail:
       Bring hailstones into the school room.
   (e) Snow:
       Examine the crystals; draw the forms on blackboard. Observe the change into water and the change of the water-drop to vapor.
   (f) (g) Sleet, Fog, Mist; as suggested by experiments. Fog and Mist are clouds near the surface of the earth.

SUGGESTIONS.

1. Do not attempt to teach more than the children can understand.
2. Require the children to bring into school the results of their own experiences and observations.
3. Give the above lessons when the weather conditions are such as to admit of actual observation of phenomena.
4. Read lessons in Normal Third Reader, relating to phenomena studied.
5. Read other descriptions, poems and stories about the phenomena studied.
6. Have frequent compositions.

BOOKS OF REFERENCE FOR TEACHERS.

Science For All.—Vol. I. Ice, Water and Steam, Air and Gas. Vol. II. How Sunshine Warms the Earth; Why the Rain Falls. Vol. III. Why the Clouds Float, and What the Clouds Say; Dew and Hoar Frost; How a Snow-flake is Formed; How Hailstones are Forged in the Clouds. Vol. IV. Fogs.

Parker's How to Teach Geography; Fry's Sand Modeling; King's Methods and Aids in Geography; Shalers' Our Continent; Paul Berts' First Steps in Science; Tyndalls' Forms of Water; Shalers' First Book in Geology; Geike's Physical Geography; Huxley's Physiography.

These books are to be found in the Teachers' Library, Franklin School.

FOURTH YEAR.

SOIL.

Take trips to Woodley Lane or to Pennsylvania Avenue extended, southeast (across the bridge).

Composition of Soil:

Note the decay of rocks that is constantly taking place.
Visit a locality where decayed rocks can be seen.
Secure specimens of such decayed rocks.
Show that the kind of soil of a vicinity depends largely on the underlying rock.
Show how the decaying vegetation aids in the formation of soil and how it affects its fertility; visit the woods for this purpose.

Agents in Soil Making:

Note the natural agents—ice, frost, air, water, etc.—that aid in soil making.
Obtain from pupils the part that the winds, floods, rivers, glaciers, lakes, oceans play in moving and grinding rocks and in distributing soil.

Kinds of Soil:

Obtain specimens of clay, sand, loam, vegetable mold, etc.
By experiment show that clay is impervious to water.
Show that gravel soils, soils made from sand stone, lime stone, etc., are permeable.
Show why soil should be kept open to admit air and water.
Show why presence of stones in soil is desirable.
Obtain from pupils the reasons for ploughing in Autumn.

Lessons to be read in connection with Soil:
Normal Fourth Reader (Lessons 3, 4, 8, 9, 13, 15, 17).

HILLS AND VALLEYS.

Visit a hill noting its shape, parts, composition (materials of which it is made.)
Mold a hill in sand. Draw a hill.
Obtain from pupils the names applied to different parts of the hill—top or summit, base, foot or bottom, slopes.
Observe that the slopes may be gradual, steep or abrupt.

Call attention to the variety in size and shape of the hills pupils have seen.

Show how the agents of denudation—the sun, frost, air, water, rain, mist, etc.—alter the size and shape of hills.

Show how the wind, brooks, vers, etc., remove the results of this action—the work of these agents. (See Soil Making).

Show that the presence of soil and grass on a hill-side helps to preserve its form.

Mold and draw a chain of hills.

Call attention to the valleys. Show that some are wide while others are deep and narrow.

Show that the softer the stone of which the hills are formed the wider will be the valleys.

Obtain from pupils the uses of hills.

Have pupils name and locate hills and chains of hills which they have seen.

Lessons to be read in connection with the study of Hills and Valleys:
Normal Fourth Reader (Lesson 5);
Geographical Reader (Lessons 2 and 3);
Swinton's Introductory Geography (Part of lesson 5);
Read also from Brooks and Brook Basins.

MOUNTAINS.

Call attention to the difference between hills and mountains.

Explain the formation of mountains.

Mold and draw a range of mountains.

Describe a volcano, an earthquake.

Name, locate and tell pupils about a few noted volcanoes.

Show that the size and forms of mountains are being constantly modified by the agents of denudation (See Hills and Valleys.)

Describe a glacier; canons.

Tell pupils about the canons of the Colorado river. Show pictures of the same.

Develop terms peak, precipice, chasm, pass, gap, gorge, ravine, plateau, etc.

Show how the cold, snowy heights aid in the condensation of vapor.

Describe the uses of mountains.

Show how mountains are represented on maps.

Name, locate and describe briefly a few mountain systems of the world.

Lessons to be read in connection with the study of mountains:
Normal Fourth Reader (Lessons 5, 6, 7, 16);
Geographical Reader (Lessons 21, 14, 4. Parts of lessons 15, 16, 17);
Swinton's Introductory Geography (Parts of lessons 5, 11, 14 (a), 15, 17, 26).

SPRINGS.

Review work of vapor in Third Grade.

Lead pupils to tell what becomes of the water that falls as rain in a clayey region.

Note the fact that part runs off in gutters and in creeks to a larger stream or river.

Show that much which is collected in pools, ponds, etc., is evaporated.

Show that plants absorb much of the moisture.

Lead pupils to see that much of the water which falls on permeable soil sinks into the earth.

Trace the underground course of water showing where it comes to the surface again, and why.

Visit a spring.

Call attention to iron springs, sulphur springs, hot springs, geysers, etc.

Have children read of the wonderful geysers of Yellowstone Park and of Iceland.

Describe a well. Lead pupils to note the difference between wells and springs.

Describe an artesian well; give its use.

Lessons to be read in connection with work on springs:
Normal Fourth Reader (Lesson 10);
Geographical Reader (Lesson 6);
Swinton's Introductory Geography (Parts of lessons 6, 24).

RIVERS.

Visit either the Potomac River or Rock Creek. * From an elevation obtain an unobstructed view of a broad stretch of country, where the pupils can see the stream and its tributaries; the valley and the smaller valleys leading into it.

Show that a river has its source in springs, lakes, etc.

Note that a river is supplied with water by brooks, creeks, rivers, springs, ponds, lakes, etc. (tributaries).

Lead pupils to discover how much land a river drains—river basin.

Show what a water parting is, and how it is formed. Don't fail to make pupils see the locations of water partings.

Show what is meant by a water-shed.

Mold a river basin.

Lead pupils to see what bounds a river basin.

Show that the size of a river basin depends on the distance the hills or mountains, in which the line of parting occurs, are from the river.

Have pupils tell why the water of a river flows.

Show the number of slopes a river basin has.

Lead pupils to see that a river basin includes all the branches of the river, and that each tributary has a basin of its own.

Show in what part of the basin the river is found.

Obtain from pupils the meaning of bed of the river, river valley, channel, banks, current, etc.

Show why rivers wind.

Lead pupils to tell on what the rapidity of a river depends.

Show on what the quantity of water of a river depends.

Show how a river bed composed of permeable strata affects the quantity of water of a river.

Show in what portion of the river's course the flow is most rapid, is the slowest, and why. (Torrent portions. Flood plains).

Lead pupils to tell why falls and rapids occur.

Show where in the river's course they occur. (Cataract portion.)

Lead pupils to see on what the color of the water of a river depends.

Obtain from pupils what becomes of the sediment carried by the river. (See Soil, Hills and Mountains.)

Show what effects floods have on a river—robbing it of portions of land along its course—spreading sediment in other portions, deepening its channel, etc.

Show uses of rivers.

Describe a canal. Give its uses.

Give much practice in finding and bounding river basins from maps.

Have pupils name and locate a few of the large rivers of the world.

Lessons to be read in connection with the study of rivers:

Normal Fourth Reader (Lessons 11 and 12);

Geographical Reader (Lessons 6, 7, 8, 9, 10, 11, 12, 13, 14);

Swinton's Introductory Geography (Parts of lessons 5, 12, 15).

COAST LINES.

Lead children to see that the line of meeting of the continent with the ocean or some arm of the sea is the coast.

Obtain from pupils the causes of waves.

Call attention to the tides—number a day—time for the ebb, and time for the flow.

Show the effects of the waves and tides on the coast.

Show children that the wearing away of the softer materials of the coast forms the bays, gulfs and other indentations.

Lead the pupils to see that the capes, points, promontories, etc., are the harder rocks of the coast which the waves have been able to affect very slowly.

(By means of sand modeling, pupils should be given proper concepts of capes, peninsulas, points, promontories, isthmuses, bays, gulfs, inlets, harbors, seas, etc.)

Have the pupils name and locate a few prominent capes, peninsulas, bays, gulfs, etc.

Lessons to be read in connection with study of the coast :

Normal Fourth Reader (Seashore. On the Cliff. Marine (sea) Pebbles);

Geographical Reader (Lesson 10);

Swinton's Introductory Geography (Lessons 4 and 5).

ISLANDS.

River Islands:

Take a trip to one or more of the islands in the Potomac River.
Show that river islands have been separated from the mainland.
Show that delta islands are formed of the soil deposited at the mouths of rivers.
Name and locate several rivers having deltas.

Continental Islands:

Show that some continental islands are formed by inroads made by the sea—the wear and tear of the winds, tides, etc.
Show that others are made by the gradual sinking of land about the coast line and the invasion of the sea.
Show that still others are formed by the rising of land from the sea.
(The plants and animals found on continental islands, together with the construction of the surface, indicate their origin.)
Name and locate many continental islands.

Oceanic Islands:

Show that many oceanic islands are formed by the subsidence of the earth's crust which has carried down bases of mountains, leaving only peaks above water.
Study briefly some of the plants and animals peculiar to these islands.
Describe coral islands (atolls).
Note their circular form and the usual presence of a lake or lagoon in their centre.
Show that they were formed by insects working on the slopes of subsiding mountains.
Obtain specimens of different kinds of coral.
Name and locate several oceanic islands.

Lessons to be read in connection with the study of islands:
Normal Fourth Reader (Lessons 12 and 14);
Geographical Reader (The West Indies, The Pacific Ocean);
Swinton's Introductory Geography (Lesson 4).

CONTINENTS.

Show that continents are great masses of land raised above the level of the ocean.
Name and give relative positions of all the continents.
Give relative sizes of the continents.

Lessons to be read in connection with the study of continents :
Normal Fourth Reader (Lessons 1, 2 and 18);
Swinton's Introductory Geography (Lessons 7 and 11).

OCEANS.

Name and give positions of the different oceans.
Give causes of the waves.
Note the facts of the tides—the number of tides each day, and the name and time of each.
Study briefly the life of the ocean, obtaining specimens when possible. Compare life in the ocean with life on the land.

Lessons to be read in connection with the study of oceans :
Normal Fourth Reader (Lesson 4. The Sea. Marine Pebbles. The Seashore);
Geographical Reader (The Atlantic Ocean, The Pacific Ocean, The Indian Ocean);
Swinton's Introductory (Geography Lesson 7).

Much other supplementary matter should be read, including books of travel, describing the character of the people and the industries of the country. Make the children understand how mines are worked, what a canal is, a lock, how goods are transported, the occupations of the people in different parts of the country, manufacturing, agriculture. Encourage the children to bring into the class pictures representing places and processes, to bring also fruits and other natural products, as well as manufactured products, when practicable. Compare other cities with Washington in size, importance and industries. Children should be made to appreciate direction and relative distance.

But little memorizing may be done. Make the children read intelligently and talk with corresponding intelligence, read connectedly and talk with corresponding unity. The children, while talking, may be led to form correct definitions of such natural divisions of land and water as pupils of this grade are expected to be able to define.

Children should be led to sketch rapidly to impress relative size and position, and to shade or color to show contour.

BOOKS OF REFERENCE FOR TEACHERS.

Science For All.—Vol. I. Hills, Dales and Valleys; Rivers, Their Work and Canon-making; Geysers; A Piece of Coal; Lakes, and How They Were Formed. Vol. II. Continental Islands, and How They Were Formed; Oceanic Islands and Their History; Glaciers, How Glaciers Move; The Story of a Volcano; A Peat Bog; The Gravel on the Garden Path; Why the Sea is Salt. Vol. III. Burnt-out Volcanoes; The Bottom of the Sea; The Scenery of the Shore; Table-lands, and How They Were Formed; Coral-islands; The Rivers of the Sea. Vol. IV. Earthquakes, How Earthquakes are Caused; A Clod of Clay; A Grain of Sand; The Wanderings of a Pebble; Cracks in the Earth's Crust. Vol. V. A Coal Field; An Iceberg; Rock-making-rhizopods.

Parker's How to Teach Geography; Fry's Sand Modeling; King's Methods and Aids in Geography; Shalers' Our Continent; Paul Berts' First Steps in Science; Tyndall's Forms of Water; Shalers' First Book in Geology; Geike's Physical Geography; Huxley's Physiography.

These books can be had at the Teachers' Library, Franklin School.

FIFTH YEAR.

Globe Lessons:

Give a series of the Globe Lessons to show the shape of the earth, and the land and water of the earth; the northern and southern hemispheres and the eastern and western hemispheres; the axes and circumference of the earth. Much practice must be given for determining the relative positions of continents and oceans which involves a knowledge of direction. The term antipodes and its application should be thoroughly taught.

NORTH AMERICA.

Location—In relation to the hemispheres and to the other continents; to the oceans.

Shape—Triangular, broad at north, tapering to the south.

Area—Greatest length and greatest breadth.

Relief and Contour—(By use of globe and maps).

Fix the main continental axis together with the eastern and western slopes. Show that this axis is out of line of the center resulting in a long slope and a short one.

Fix the secondary axis and eastern and western slopes.

Follow the eastern slope of the primary highlands and the western slope of the secondary highlands to their line of meeting, fixing river beds.

Follow slopes to line of meeting with the oceans fixing the coast.

Study coast lines noting only prominent projections and indentations of each coast.

(The molding of the continent in sand, both by the teacher and by the pupils, should accompany all of the work required above and much of that that follows. The general contour of the continent should be impressed by means of much map drawing.)

Locate the Rocky Mountain System and the Appalachian System.

Note the great extent of the Western Highlands; the different ranges of which they are composed; the great length and unbroken character of these ranges; the various heights of the plateau on which they rest; height of some of the most important peaks; character of plateaus between ranges; the noted parks and valleys, minerals, etc.

Compare the Eastern with the Western Highlands.

Note the difference in height, length, and general character of ranges and valleys. Name and give height of a few prominent peaks.

Locate and describe the Great Central Plain and the Atlantic Plain.

Pictures, specimens and descriptions obtained from books of travel; the Geographical Reader and the Geography are valuable aids in forming correct mental pictures of the relief of the continent.

Excellent subjects for composition are afforded by this work.

Locate the Gulf of Mexico and Arctic Ocean Divide.

Locate the Northen Swell.

Fix the great river basins of the continent, the Mississippi Basin, the Mackenzie Basin, the St. Lawrence Basin, the Saskatchewan Basin, the Hudson Bay Basin; the drainage of the Atlantic, the Pacific, the Gulf of Mexico and Arctic Slopes.

Study the most important of these basins respecting water-divide boundaries; relative size of basin drained; main river of system; tributaries; source slope; general character of rivers of the basin, whether navigable or not, whether adapted to commerce or manufacture; chief cities located on the rivers, why located, where they are; history connected with rivers of basin, etc. (See outline for "Rivers" under Fourth Grade).

Let the description of rivers or river basins form the subject for compositions.

Political Divisions:

Name and locate the political divisions of North America.

Study each in relation to extent, ownership, form of government, chief occupation of people, important cities, etc.

United States:

Study representative States carefully.
Study from six to ten cities in detail.

In connection with these study the water and the railroad routes of the country.

Let the children read to know more of people than of boundaries of States ; more of the industries of the people ; more of the products of different sections of the country ; the means of transportation ; the centres of trade, etc.

Lead the children to see sequence in the study of geography, and do not overwhelm them with details, especially in political geography. Connect as much history as possible with all geographical study.

Make use of the National Museum and Zoological Gardens and let the life, natural products and manufactured products of different sections be represented in the class when practicable. The process by which natural products are made valuable and become articles of commerce should be considered.

Maps :

The rapid sketching of maps at first from copy and then from memory should be practised to fix coast lines. Drainage of the continent should be represented by the mountains forming the chief water partings together with the rivers whose beds are formed by the meeting of main slopes. No time need be spent in beautifying these maps. Outline maps may be profitably used for representation of productions, political divisions, location, of cities, railroads, etc.

SOUTH AMERICA.

(By use of the globe and maps.)

Comparison with North America lightens the study of this continent, and gives value to information.

Location—In relation to hemispheres ; to other continents ; to oceans.

Area—Greatest length and breadth.

Note the similarity in general shape ; in location of primary and secondary axes ; in length and direction of slopes ; in location of river basins, etc.

Model and draw as in North America.

Study a few of the plants, animals, and minerals of the

continent. The study of these furnishes excellent subjects for compositions.

Locate and give brief descriptions of the political divisions.

Swinton's Introductory Geography and Scribner's Geographical Reader should be used mainly as reading books. Encourage pupils to do much supplementary reading.

Teachers will find the following books very helpful to a successful presentation of this subject:

†Guyot's Earth and Man.
*Parker's How to Study Geography.
†Frye's Geography with Sand Modeling.
†Ritter's Comparative Geography.
†Guyot's Physical and Common School Geographies.
†Physiography—Huxley.
†Shaler's First Book of Geology and The Story of Our Continent.
†Geike's Physical Geography.
†King's Methods and Aids in Geography.
†Elderton's Maps and Map Drawing.

SIXTH YEAR.

Study Europe, Asia, Africa and Australia.

In the study of these continents, follow the plan given for North America in fifth grade.

Compare size, form, length and direction of axes; length and direction of slopes, coast lines, drainage, etc., of each continent with those already studied.

Only leading countries require detailed study.

A few important cities in each country should be studied, and in connection with these, water and railroad routes should be learned. Study the relation of these countries and cities to one another, and to the United States in manufactures and commerce.

---

*Found on the teacher's desk.
†Found in the teacher's library at the Franklin School.

The National Museum should be visited, pictures and objects representing the life and condition of the people should be brought into class, and studied and compared by the children when practicable.

The different forms of government should be understood in general by the children.

Much valuable work may be done by a comparison of the sizes of countries; of the industries of countries; of conditions of people; of numbers of people; of modes of life, etc.

Globe Lessons:

Pupils should mould in clay a sphere representing the globe. They should indicate thereon parallels, meridians, zones, hemispheres, continents and oceans. They should be led with sphere in hand to represent hemispheres, continents and oceans on the blackboard or paper. Teach longitude and time.

Children should be encouraged to read much on the topics Plants, Animals, Races of Mankind, States of Society. Articles of dress, warfare, agriculture, etc., representing the life of different races of mankind, may be exhibited, examined, and compared, if practicable.

Maps— Maps should be modeled in sand to show relief of continents and drawn to impress contour, position and direction of rivers, locations of important cities. No time need be spent in beautifying these maps.

Do not burden children with details of boundaries and areas. Let them study conditions, relations and sequence, and while studying these, let them refer constantly to maps.

Reference books for teachers are the same as for fifth grade, all of which are to be found either on the teacher's desk, or in the Teacher's Library, Franklin School.

SEVENTH YEAR.

The work of this grade is largely a study of maps, Text must be read and studied for explanation of what the maps disclose. The logic for the existence of one set of facts disclosed by the maps—political geography—must be sought in the other sets of facts disclosed—mathematical geography and physical geography—by the same maps or by others used for the purpose.

1. By use of the globe and other apparatus study the mathematical geography given in Swinton's Common School Geography. In this connection, consult *Elderton's Maps and Map Drawing*.

2. Study the location of North America with respect to its position on the globe and also to the other continents and to the great water divisions of the earth. Get a clear idea of the general features of the coast lines (including adjacent islands) tracing the cause of each great indentation far back into the interior.

3. Determine where settlements would be made first *naturally*. Study the history (geographically) of the first discoveries and the first settlements. (Do not make these too numerous—a half dozen each of discoveries and of settlements are enough.)

4. Study the political divisions of North America. · Locate each accurately with respect to bodies of water, and mountain ranges, and to the other divisions of the continent. Learn the leading facts of history respecting the fixing of the boundary lines of the divisions of the continent.

5. Study the climate of the several divisions (see Swinton, p. 9), and determine by conversation and reading the general character of the flora, the fauna, the productions and the industries of each. Determine where commercial centers would naturally be developed, remembering that the means of commercial intercourse was at first chiefly by water.

6. Study the United States as a whole, with respect to its position on the continent; its size (absolute and relative); its climate; its productions; its industries, etc.; its historic relations with the other divisions of the continent; its commercial relation with other parts of the continent. This will involve the definite location of centers of commerce and trade (not more than twenty need be studied, but each must be fixed definitely in position, and the relative time of the beginning of its development must be known), and routes of travel and means of communication. Study to know about the legal regulations controlling commercial intercourse between the divisions of the continent. (These laws are not to be even read in

detail, but the child should know that commerce is governed, and should know the machinery by which it is governed, in what cities the United States has consuls, what a consul's duty is, who appoints him, in what cities of the United States other nations of the continent have consuls.)

Locate every city exactly, and know how products get to it, and by what means products are taken away from it.

7. Study important centers of trade (not more than ten besides those already studied) within the United States. Show why each is located, where it is, (climate, bodies of water, mountain ranges, fertile valleys, etc., etc., etc.) Study size, characteristics and relative importance. Definite location and means of access are to be known and understood. Each city studied should be associated with the State of which it is a part, and with the group of States of which its State forms a part.

8. Study the governments of the various countries of North America. This will involve a study of the divisions of each, but not to the extent that the names and boundaries of each division may be remembered. Study the functions of each subordinate part in the general government. Study how each government is represented in the other governments of the continent.

SOUTH AMERICA.

1. Study South America first, to locate it on the globe, and then to locate it definitely with respect to other grand divisions of the earth, and the great bodies of water. (Use globe and maps freely.)

2. Study the location of different states, their climate and productions in a general way.

3. Study to know the commercial relations the United States have with South America. Locate definitely from six to a dozen commercial centres, determine those things for which each is noted and why it is so characterized, with what centres of trade in the United States each has communication, and exactly how each is reached from such centres in the United States.

4. Study in a general way the governments of South America, comparing them with that of our own.

Learn where our government has representatives (definitely locate); what governments are represented in our country— where (definitely locate).

5. Study the customs and character of the people of the various countries in comparison with those of our own people.

EUROPE.

In a way corresponding to that in which South America has been studied, study Europe, Asia, Africa and Australia. Europe will require as much study and effort as Asia, Africa and Australia combined.

The different countries in Europe should be studied relatively, according to the importance of our commercial relations with them. (At least one city in each country should be studied). This relativity is one thing the teacher must strive to have the child know and understand.

The amount of "place geography" must be kept down to the minimum, but what is attempted must be learned with great definiteness. The child must know exactly where a city or country is, why Americans want to go there, and how they can get there.

Learn the most important coaling stations for the United States Navy, where they are, why these places were chosen, and how to get to them.

EIGHTH YEAR.

PHYSICAL GEOGRAPHY.

Temperature:

Why does it become colder as one goes north or south from the equator?

Why are the extremes of temperature greater in the interior of a continent than near its shores? Why are the winters colder and the summers hotter?

Why does it become colder as one rises above the earth's surface?

Rainfall:

What is evaporation?
Can hot air or cold air retain a greater quantity of moisture?
Can rare air or dense air retain the greater quantity of moisture?
What are clouds and fog?
What produces rainfall?
Why is dew deposited at night?
What produces snow and hail?

Air Currents:

What causes the wind to blow?
What are the trade winds and what causes them?
What produces the land and the sea breezes at the seashore?
What produces whirlwinds and cyclones?
What is the Signal Service?
Whence is the information given obtained and how are conclusions reached?
Of what benefit is the Signal Service?
What is the cause of the tides of the ocean?
What causes currents in the ocean?
What effects are produced by them?
What effect do physical conditions and relative position have on climate? How do these affect industries and the life of the people?

Much systematic reading should be done by the pupils, the foregoing list of topics serving as a guide for the same.

Pupils should be trained to talk in connected discourse upon each of the subjects suggested.

Take as a guide, in the work given above, Chapters IV, V, VI, IX, X and XXI of the Eclectic Physical Geography.

U. S. History.

FIFTH YEAR.

1. The Saxons in Denmark.
2. Britain.
3. The Saxons in Britain.
4. Union of Saxon Kingdoms; King Alfred.
5. The Northmen in France; the Normans in England.
6. Growth of the Country; Magna Charta.
7. Customs of the people and conditions of civilization; buildings, modes of life, laws, etc., etc.; compare with those of the Britains, the early Saxons and the Normans.
8. Columbus; who he was, what he did.
9. America; its place, its condition.
10. The Indians; compare with early Saxons; modes of life, general character, etc., etc.
11. Virginia.
12. New York.
13. New England.
14. Pennsylvania.
15. Maryland.
16. Growth of the country; habits of the people; compare with Saxons, Normans, Indians.
17. The Colonies; by whom governed; why? life of the people; growth of freedom and independence.
18. The Revolution.
19. George Washington.
20. Read much for better understanding; talk much for expression and for better understanding; preserve in all a connected outline of general facts, from the invasion of Britain by the Saxons to the present time. The pupil should have, beside his regular reading book, access to Yonge's History of England, Dickens's Young Folks' History of England, Phillips's Historical Readers 1, 2, 3 and 4, Hawthorne's True Stories of

History and Biography, Fisk's Washington and His Country, Longfellow's Hiawatha, and Miles Standish.

The teacher should consult McMaster, to be found in the seventh grade schools; also Green's History of the English People, in the Teachers' Library at the Franklin School.

SIXTH YEAR.

The historical course in this grade covers four periods—that of discovery, that of settlement, that of colonization and that of the revolution. It is important that the children be led to an intelligent study of the life of these periods, of the men who best represent them and of the geography necessary to a good understanding of the history. This geography should be made as graphic as possible. All reading and study should be done with the maps at hand for ready reference.

The following topics are suggested:

Discoveries and Explorations:

European commercial activity in the fifteenth century.

The invention of the mariner's compass.

The life of Columbus, including his nativity, early life and character; the geographic ideas of his time; the views of Columbus; his patrons; his voyages and the results of them.

Give a brief account of the following discoverers, locating the scenes of their discoveries: The Cabots, Amerigo Vespucci, Ponce de Leon, Balboa, Verrazani, Cartier, DeSoto, Champlain, Hudson.

It is important that a few locations should be known exactly by the child, and that the relation of these locations to the continent at large be discussed and understood.*

---

*NOTE.—The outline here given may be enlarged at the discretion of the teacher. The outline adopted should be adhered to and should be thoroughly fixed in the memories of the pupils. Much outside reading is expected. Many incidents of interest will be noted. Much detail will be read and talked about in class. The teacher must see that all these are properly associated by the child, not only respecting time and locality and results, but also respecting their importance. These details must not prevent the thorough fixing of the sequential outline. They will, if properly treated, make the main facts more prominent and more important.

Settlements:

Study brief biographies of Walter Raleigh, John Smith, Peter Minuit, Lord Baltimore and Lord Clarendon. Study the nativities and general characters of these men, their objects in founding colonies, whether to find an escape from religious or political persecution, or for purposes of gain or proprietorship. Tell from whom the founders obtained their grants; the character of the governments established; the character and conditions of the settlers.

Teach the main facts of the Virginia, Maryland, New England, Dutch, Pennsylvania, and the Southern Settlements.

The colonial settlements should be grouped so that their relations to each other in their early development may be clearly understood. It is profitable to teach these settlements by groups whose parts are related by character of people or by legal considerations. The chronological order of settlements may be learned as reviews or as cross-section work.*

Colonial:

Study the growth of the colonies. Study how their prosperity was affected by legislation, the character of the settlers, the Indian wars and the Colonial wars. Learn what each nationality contributed to the country. Study the life in the colonies with reference to Education, Industries, Commerce, Literature and Religion. (Consult McMaster.)

The work upon the Revolution may be done by learning the biographies of *Patrick Henry, Washington, Franklin, Samuel Adams and Alexander Hamilton;* by studying the following topics in their relation; or both courses may be taken. This

---

*NOTE.—The pupils are expected to read much outside of their regular text-books, and to talk much in class of details and of interesting incidents. For the value and proper use of these details see *note* under discoveries. The geographical part of the outline must be definitely fixed in the child's memory.

The colonial wars should be learned as developments of the study of the conditions of the settlers, and the circumstances attending their lives in the new country; the character of the country; the character and rights or supposed rights of the Indians and their mode of warfare; the claims of nations, etc. Few details should be learned except those of the French and Indian war that resulted in fixing boundaries, and other localities that have permanent geographic importance.

work involves wide reading. In all reading and study of history let the geography be a constant companion.

The Revolution—Topics Suggested:
The Navigation Acts.
The Stamp Act.
The Assemblies of Virginia and Massachusetts.
The Congress of 1765.
The Boston Massacre.
The Boston Port Bill.
Lexington.
The Declaration of Independence.
The situation in New York, New Jersey and Pennsylvania.
Burgoyne's Surrender.
The War in the South.
The Treaty with France.
The Siege of Yorktown.
Lafayette.
The Naval Battles.
The Close of the War.
The Treaty of Peace.
The formation of States.
The formation of the Constitution.

The teacher is referred to what is said about details in teaching Discoveries and Settlements.

SEVENTH YEAR.

1. Review the prominent facts of the Revolution. The contemporaneous history of the period of the Revolution should constitute the chief work of this review. This will lead to an understanding of the motives of the colonists and to the true character of the Revolution.

2. Give emphasis to the struggle in the formation of the Constitution, and to the general character of that instrument.

3. Study the financial situation of the country at the time of the formation of the Government.

For the Period Succeeding the Revolution Study:

1. The establishment of Government, Departments, etc.
2. Establishment of a Seat of Government.
3. The acquisition of territory and the admission of States; the growth of States.
4. The growth of population; the sources of population.
5. Inventions; the growth of industries; the growth of industrial appliances.
6. The growth of commerce and the means of transportation.
7. The administrations and the leading events of each.
8. The wars, their causes and their results.
9. As much of representative persons as is practicable.

While studying the administrations the growth of the country should be a leading topic for careful consideration. The children should be made interested in changes that have taken place in population; in the growth of territory; in the administration of States; in the development of growth of centers of population; in the development of new industries; in processes of industry; in means of communication and transportation; in the development of schools, newspapers, etc., etc. This is the opportunity for training pupils to read intelligently and for a definite purpose; this the opportunity to give pupils broad outlooks on the related institutions of our common society.

The pupils of this grade are old enough to understand contemporaneous history; the important causes of changes in modes of industry, the effects of invention; in general, the sequence of events. With these thoughts in mind the teacher will cause much reading to be done, and will make every effort possible to have such reading done in a way to make it profitable rather than confusing and dissipating. A clear, sequential outline should be referred to with persistent frequency to determine the place and the relative importance of all that is read, and of every conversation.

It is most difficult for some minds to appreciate the relative importance of historical events, anecdotes, individual eccentricities, etc., etc. Good teaching will not avoid these, but will give to them only the importance they deserve. (See notes under Discoveries and Settlements, Sixth Grade work.)

EIGHTH YEAR.

I.

A. The Defects in the Articles of Confederation.
B. Arguments in favor of a Constitution.
C. Ratification of the Constitution.

   (a) Arguments *pro* and *con*.
   (b) Development of parties.
   (c) History of parties.

The Constitution should be thoroughly studied in connection with the outline. The pupil is expected to commit to memory very little of the Constitution. He is not expected to know the whereabouts of provisions by Article and Section, but should be able to give classified lists of such provisions, and should be able to give an intelligent explanation of each and its practical application. Much intelligent conversation is required to do this part of the work well.

II.

A. State Government:

   (a) Departments.
   (b) Elections.
   (c) Law-making.
   (d) Representative Districts.
   (e) Voters (eligibility).

B. Other Units of Government, as; County, Town, City.
C. Representation in Congress:

   Senators, Representatives.
   Conventions, Caucuses, Delegates.

III.

Comparison of the conditions of the country at the time of the organization of the Government with those now existing.

A. Territory:

   (a) Extent.
   (b) Acquisitions, whence and how obtained.
   (c) Admissions.
   (d) Government of territories; conditions of admission.

B. Inhabitants:

(a) Immigration, whence, character, extent.
(b) Consequent changes in the habits, character and sentiments of the people.
(c) Naturalization Laws.
(d Effect on the size of Congress; when changes in the number of Representatives have been made.

C. 1.—Industries:

(a) Inventions.
(b) Natural Products.
(c) Manufactures.

2.—Transportation:

Oxen, Horses and Mules, Turnpikes, Canals, Steamboats, Railroads, Express.

3.—Communication:

(a) Postal Service; changes in the rates of postage.
(b) Express.
(c) Telegraph.
(d) Telephone.

4.—Tendency of Population—(Why?)—Effects of this Tendency.
5.—Centres of Population—Location—Leading Causes.

D. Conditions of Living:

(a) Newspapers.
(b) Books.
(c) Schools.
(d) Churches.
(e) Society.
(f) Conveniences and appliances.

E. Modes of Living.

General Remarks on the Study of Nature.

A very common complaint against some of the work of the modern school is of the large number and variety of subjects prescribed for study. It is urged that the learner's mind is confused and dissipated by the frequent turning from one subject to another, and that because of this fragmentary method of study he fails in his grasp of the parts of any subject in a sequentially arranged entirety.

In too many instances the complaint is well founded. There is ground for such adverse criticism whenever an attempt is made to teach more than the so-called common branches of learning unless the instruction proceeds from an understanding of the relation of educational endeavor to the sum of knowledge and also to those processes of mental activity by which human knowledge is increased, applied, and conserved. It is necessary to understand the correlation of the various branches of common knowledge as means of educative processes and also the relative values of branches of common knowledge as ends of educational endeavor.

A determination of the first part of this subject requires a knowledge of how the mind grows and of how it acquires facts.

Only by an understanding of the correlative values of educational processes can educational energies be conserved and made productive of most good. The study of plants in the lower grades of school is made delightful and profitable when it is prescribed, not to give the learner a knowledge of botany, not for giving him botanical facts, but as a means of training him to see, as a means of getting related information for the learning and exercise of exact expression and the correct use of language, and for making verbal material that has meaning to the child for his first reading lessons.

The teaching of the facts of the forms and habits of animals will never serve to crowd a course of instruction if it is done that the learner may be trained in methods of getting knowledge and in the use of idiom in formulating such knowledge, and if it be remembered at the same time that it is not the purpose of this work to teach zoology.

Teaching some of the simpler elements of chemistry, and of the simpler fundamental laws of physics, the facts and laws of nature cannot be considered as imposing an extra burden on the children by him who sees in these facts and laws, the beginning steps that must be taken if the child is to be made to understand the description and causes of geographic phenomena he will soon be expected to learn. That a walk to the fields, to the hill-top, or to the river-side, takes him from the spelling lesson, or from the writing lesson, or from the reading lesson, is true, but in the end such walk saves much time if the right use is made of it. This can be made to appear if correct products are estimated when a balance is struck.

Elementary lessons in plants, animals, chemistry, physics, physical geography and other branches of common knowledge become a necessity to the teacher who understands why the child is in school, what a teacher's duty is toward his pupil, and how such duty can be discharged, not only most profitably, but also most easily, most economically, as well as most intelligently. He who has made a successful study of the relativity of the processes of mind development, together with a mastery of the logical sequences in the growth and development of subjects which the child must learn in his school course, and who will at the same time instruct his pupils in the light of such information can never have a crowded course of study. Where such teaching is found a crowded course of study does not exist because it can not. A child thus taught will not be crammed, will not be overburdened by variety of subjects to be studied, will never be confused by change of subjects, or embarrassed by the use of facts in their wrong places.

Children thus taught are not confused when examined, or

wakeful when they should sleep, because of overburdened brains.

The teacher must remember that a knowledge of botany is not the primary, nor hardly a secondary purpose in giving plant lessons in the lower grades of school; that teaching zoology is not the primary purpose of giving animal lessons; that a knowledge of the science of chemistry, or the science of physics, or of physiology, is not contemplated by giving elementary lessons in these branches of learning.

Plant Work.

FIRST YEAR.

SEEDS.

Recognize, name and describe from six to a dozen common seeds, as; beans, rice, peas, corn, oats, wheat, coffee, etc.

Plant many seeds of one kind to furnish specimens for class work.

Plant a few seeds of each of several varieties to establish fact that each seed contains a living germ.

Show by experiments that moisture, light and heat are necessary conditions for the healthy development of a plant.

Plant seeds in cotton that the different stages of germination may be observed.

Study the parts of the seed with the corresponding parts of the growing plant to establish facts of origin.

Encourage children to plant seeds at home, to note time needed for appearance of plants and for their final development.

Develop and write many stories about seeds to be read by the children.

Read interesting stories from standard authors to be reproduced orally by the children.

PLANT.

Study the plant as a whole, naming, locating and giving uses of its parts; roots, stem and leaves.

The wild flowering plants of the vicinity should furnish specimens for this work.

Experiment to show uses of each part of the plant.

LEAVES.

Recognize and name from six to a dozen common leaves and tell on what each grew.

Draw, and describe each of the leaves selected, noting size, shape, color and texture (what the child can see).

Appropriately color each drawing.

Note whether margins of the selected leaves are entire or cut.

Note the venation of the leaves studied.

Discover what the veins contain and whence this juice comes.

Invent and write many stories about leaves for the children to read.

Read beautiful stories of leaves from standard authors to be reproduced orally by the children.

FLOWERS.

Recognize and name from six to a dozen common flowers.

Tell whether the flowers selected grew on tree, bush or other plant.

Note the size, shape and color of the flowers studied.

Discover the two cups of the flower.

Note whether the outer and inner cups consist of one part or of many parts, respectively.

Draw attention to the thread-like parts in the centre of the flower.

Describe and draw the flowers studied.

Color appropriately each drawing.

Make and write many stories on flowers to be read by children.

Read stories on flowers from standard authors to be reproduced orally by children.

FRUIT.

Name and describe from six to a dozen different fruits.

Draw the fruits described and color appropriately each drawing.

The apple, pear, peach or cherry, grape and acorn are suggested.

Outline for study of the apple :
1. What it is and where it grows.
2. Covering—color.
3. Size and shape.
4. Dimples—(a) stem, (b) eye.
5. Parts (a) Skin—color, texture, use.
       (b) Pulp—color, cells, juice, use.
       (c) Core—number of parts, use.
6. Seeds—color, parts, use.
7. Uses.

Follow a corresponding outline for each of the other fruits studied.

Compare the fruits studied.

Develop and write many descriptions of fruits to be read by the children.

Read stories on fruit from standard authors to be reproduced orally by the children.

In each lesson every child should have one or more specimens, otherwise the work should not be done.

SECOND YEAR.

SEEDS.

Name, recognize and describe from six to a dozen common seeds, as ; beans, rice, corn, oats, wheat, coffee, etc.

Plant many seeds of one kind to furnish specimens for class work.

Plant a few seeds of each of several varieties to establish fact that each seed contains a living germ.

Show by experiments that moisture, light and heat are necessary conditions for the healthy development of a plant.

Plant seed in cotton that the different stages of germination may be observed.

Study the parts of the seed—seed-coat, seed-leaves and germ.

Compare the parts of the seed with the corresponding part of the growing plant to establish facts of origin.

Encourage children to plant seeds at home and to note time needed for appearance of plants and their final development.

Develop and write many descriptions on seeds to be read by the children.

Read beautiful stories on seeds from standard authors to be reproduced orally by the children. Train the children in correct English.

THE PLANT.

Study the plant as a whole, naming, locating and giving uses of its parts—roots, stems, leaves.

Show by experiment uses of each part.

ROOTS.

Distinguish between fibrous and fleshy roots.

Recognize, name and describe from four to six fleshy roots, as; beets, turnips, radishes, carrots, parsnips, etc.

Draw the roots described, and color appropriately each drawing.

Note the size, shape, color and use of each root described.

Note likenesses and differences between the several fleshy roots studied.

Note likenesses and differences between fleshy and fibrous roots.

Develop and write many stories on roots for children to read.

Read stories on roots from standard authors for oral reproduction.

STEMS.

Recognize, name and describe erect, climbing and running stems. Find examples under each.

Distinguish between woody stems and juicy stems.

Find and name several plants having woody stems and several having juicy stems.

Study the shapes of stems—round, triangular and square—and find several examples of each.

Invent and write stories about stems to be read by children.

Read stories about stems for oral reproduction.

LEAVES.

Recognize, name and draw from ten to twenty common leaves and tell on what each grew.

Appropriately color each drawing made.

Describe each of the selected leaves noting size, color, shape and texture (what the child sees).

Study the parts of the leaf—the blade and the foot-stalk.

Study the apex, margin and base of each of the leaves described.

Note the venation of leaves studied, and distinguish between the frame work and the filling.

Discover what the veins contain, and whence this juice comes.

Observe likenesses and differences of leaves studied.

Invent and write many stories of leaves to be read by the children.

Read beautiful stories about leaves from good authors to be reproduced by the children.

FLOWERS.

Recognize and name from ten to twenty common flowers.

Tell whether the flowers selected grew on a tree, bush or other plant.

Note the size, shape, color and arrangement of the flowers studied.

Discover the two cups of the flower, note their relative position and name the parts of which each is composed.

Note whether the petals and sepals are united or not.

Discover and name the stamens and pistil.

Describe and draw the flowers studied.

Color appropriately each drawing.

Observe likenesses and differences between flowers selected.

Make and write many stories of flowers to be read by the children.

Read stories about flowers from standard authors to be reproduced by children.

In each lesson every child should have one or more specimens, otherwise the work should not be done.

THIRD YEAR.

LEAVES.

Name and draw from ten to twenty common leaves and tell on what each grew.

Appropriately color each drawing.

Name and define the parts of the leaf—blade, footstalk and stipules.

Observe the size, color, shape and texture of the leaves studied.

Study the apex, margin and base of each of the leaves described.

Distinguish between parallel-veined leaves and net-veined leaves. Find and name many illustrations under each.

Distinguish between feather-veined leaves and palmately-veined leaves. Find and name many illustrations of each.

Distinguish between simple leaves and compound leaves. Find and name many illustrations of each.

Distinguish between leaves and leaflets, and between leaf-stalks and branches.

Make full descriptions of each leaf studied.

Observe likenesses and differences between the leaves studied.

Read beautiful stories about leaves from standard authors to be reproduced by children.

FLOWERS.

Name and draw from ten to twenty common flowers.

Color appropriately each drawing.

Note the size, shape, color and arrangement of the flowers studied.

Name and locate the parts of the flower—corolla, calyx, stamens, pistil.

Name and define the petals and sepals.

Distinguish between monopetalous flowers and polypetalous flowers. Find and name many illustrations of each.

Study the parts of the stamen—stalk and pollen—and the parts of the pistil—stalk and seed vessel.

Note the union of stamens, also the union of pistils, in many flowers. Find and name flowers whose stamens or pistils are united.

Study a few flowers under Compositæ.

Describe in full the flowers studied.

Observe likenesses and differences between the flowers selected.

Read stories about flowers from standard authors to be reproduced by the children.

BUDS.

Note when and where on the plant buds first appear.

Distinguish between side (axillary) buds and end (terminal) buds.

Observe the scar below each axillary bud and discover what it indicates.

Note the various outer coats of the buds studied and give their uses.

Note the different ways in which the leaves are folded within the buds.

Distinguish between leaf buds and flower buds.

Note when buds swell and open.

Describe many buds.

Observe likenesses and differences between buds studied.

Draw the buds and appropriately color the drawings.

Invent and write many stories about buds to be read by the children.

Read stories about buds from standard authors for reproduction.

In each lesson each child should have one or more specimens, otherwise the work should not be done.

FOURTH YEAR.

FLOWERS.

Name, draw and describe from ten to twenty flowers including many fruit blossoms.
Color appropriately each drawing made.
Name and define the parts of the flower—calyx (sepals), corolla (petals), stamens and pistil.
Define monopetalous and polypetalous flowers, monosepalous and polysepalous flowers.
Find and name many examples of each.
Study the parts of the stamens and discover use of the pollen.
Note whether stamens are united or not.
Study the parts of the pistil and watch the development of fruit from the ovary.
Note whether pistils are united or not.
Study perfect and imperfect flowers, complete flowers, symmetrical and unsymmetrical flowers.
Find and name examples of each kind.
Note arrangement of the flowers studied.
Read many stories about flowers from standard authors for reproduction.
Read and memorize a few short, appropriate poems on flowers.
Comparisons of flowers studied.

FRUIT.

Name and describe many fruits.
Draw the fruits described and color appropriately each drawing.
Study each kind of fleshy fruit, as; the grape, lemon, orange, cucumber, apple, etc.
Study stone fruits, as; cherry, peach, plum, blackberry, raspberry, etc.
Study a few dry fruits, as; nuts, grain, etc.
Study uses of fruit described.
Observe likenesses and differences between the different fruits studied.

Read many stories about fruit from standard authors for reproduction.

Read and memorize a few short, appropriate poems on fruit.

In every lesson each child should have one or more specimens, otherwise the work should not be done.

Outline for work on the orange :

Shape—spherical

Color—orange

Surface—curved smooth or rough circles on surface—prick circles

Rind—color of inside
    texture of outside—firm
    texture of inside—soft, fibrous
    sacs in outer rind—shape, contents, uses
    relation of circles on outside to these sacs
    uses

Pulp—creases from end to end
    number of segments in each half
    shape of segments—straight inner edge, curved outer edge
    covering of segments—color—texture
    cells—color, size, shape (spindle), direction, contents (sweet or sour), arrangement, uses

Seeds—position in segments
    attachment
    seed coats—number, color, texture
    food cups
    root
    uses of seeds, rind and pulp to man
    layers of oil sacs help make rind water-proof

Experiments—squeeze rind over flame } draw conclusions
    squeeze rind into water
    squeeze juice of cells into water } draw conclusions
    squeeze juice of cells over flame

Animal Work.

FIRST YEAR.

INSECTS.

Obtain live specimens of various insects common to this vicinity. The grasshopper, butterfly, katy-did, fly, moth, dragon-fly, are suggested.

The insects selected form most excellent subjects for many of the early conversational lessons. They should be liberated after use.

Make collections of larvæ of various insects. Feed with the leaves of the same kind of tree or bush from which they were obtained.

The spinning of the cocoon, and the perfect insect which later emerges from it, should be noted by the child.

Appropriate stories, poems and songs should be given pupils in connection with insect work.

BIRDS.

Interest children in the birds of this vicinity, in their homes, in the time of their earliest appearance, etc.

Study the robin or sparrow, the duck or goose, the hen. Work with the specimen before the child.

Avoid entering too much into detail in these descriptions. Seek rather to impress upon the children the adaptation of structure of the animal to use and to environment.

Note the likenesses and differences between the duck and the goose; between the duck and the hen. Compare and contrast the feet and the bills of the hen and duck and draw conclusions.

Invent and write many short descriptions and stories about the animals studied, to be read by the children.

Read stories on animals from standard authors to be reproduced orally by the children.

Encourage the children to draw the animals studied or at least to draw characteristic parts of each.

MAMMALS.

Study the cat, dog, squirrel, rabbit, mouse, horse and fox. Work with the specimen before the child when practicable.

The remarks given under Birds apply to the study of these animals.

SECOND YEAR.

INSECTS.

Study the grasshopper, bee, butterfly or moth, and fly.

Note the parts, habits, uses and food of each.

Draw the insects studied and color appropriately each drawing.

Emphasize the adaptation of parts to uses and habits.

Interest the children in searching for the homes of insects studied; in watching the method used in obtaining food; in noting what becomes of them in winter, etc.

Make collections of the larvæ of the butterfly and moth. Feed with the leaves of the plant on which they were found. Let children watch the spinning of the cocoon and note the time which elapses between that and the appearance of the perfect insect.

Observe likenesses and differences between the different insects studied.

Develop and write many short descriptions and narrations to be read by the children.

Stories and poems by standard authors should be read to the children for oral reproduction.

Each child should be provided with a specimen of the insect studied. Use live specimens when practicable.

BIRDS.

Study the duck, hen, hawk, crane, robin and blue-bird.

Note under each the size, shape, covering, parts, habits, uses and food.

Characteristic parts and habits should receive most attention.

Adaptation of parts to mode of life should be a prominent feature in each description.

Study the likenesses and differences between the birds named and draw conclusions.

Compare and contrast corresponding characteristic parts and draw conclusions.

Other swimmers, waders, scratchers, birds of prey, etc., should be named. The Zoological Garden and the Museum can be used to an advantage in this work.

Develop and write many short descriptions and stories to be read by the children.

From outline or questions have children write many descriptions and narrations of birds.

Read interesting stories about birds from standard authors to be reproduced by children.

Have children draw the birds studied and color appropriately each drawing.

Draw characteristic parts of each bird.

Work with specimen of the bird studied before the children.

THIRD YEAR.

INSECTS.

Study the bee, beetle and grasshopper.

Every child should be provided with a specimen of the insect studied. Children should make their own collections of insects.

Not only should the structure of these insects be studied but their habits, homes, food, time of appearance, winter abode, etc., should be made subjects of interest to the child.

In the study of bees, secure specimens, if possible, of the different kinds, of honey-comb, of bee bread, etc.

Set children to search for the grubs of beetles, for young grasshoppers.

Let the study of adaptation of structure to uses and mode of living be made a strong feature of the work.

Observe likenesses and differences between the insects studied and draw conclusions.

Develop and write many descriptions and narrations of the insects studied.

Many descriptions and narrations should be written by the children from outline or questions.

Interesting stories in both prose and verse about insects, from standard authors, should be read to the children for reproduction.

Draw each insect studied and color appropriately each drawing.

SPIDERS.

Have children make collection of spiders.

Study the parts, habits, uses, adaptation of parts to mode of living, etc.

Observe likenesses and differences between spiders and two or more insects studied and draw conclusions.

Have children observe the structure and shape of the spider's web.

If possible let them watch the spider while spinning its web.

Develop and write many descriptions and narrations of spiders to be read by the children.

Have children write many descriptions and narrations from outlines or questions.

Read many stories in prose and verse about spiders from standard authors for reproduction. A few of the short poems should be memorized.

Draw spiders studied and color appropriately each drawing.

The use of the magnifying glass will add greatly to the interest of the work.

GNAWERS.

Study the squirrel, rabbit, mouse, rat, beaver, and prairie-dog.

Work with the live specimen before the children when possible, otherwise use mounted specimens.

The parts of each animal should be noted, considering more in detail characteristic parts.

Emphasize adaptation of structure to use and environment.

The habits of these animals, the food they eat and how obtained, the homes they construct, the provision they make for the winter, their life during the cold season, etc., should be dwelled upon in this study.

The different animals of the group should be compared and contrasted, and conclusions drawn.

Have the children name other gnawers. Use the Zoological Garden and Museum in this work.

Develop and write many descriptions and stories of gnawers to be read by the children.

Have children write descriptions and narrations from outline or questions.

Read appropriate stories in prose and verse about gnawers from standard authors to be reproduced by the children. The short poems should be memorized.

The animals studied should be drawn by the children, or at least characteristic parts should be drawn. Color appropriately each drawing.

FROGS AND TOADS.

Study the frog, toad and treetoad.

Secure specimens of each animal studied.

Keep specimens of the tadpole before the children so that the development of the toad or frog may be seen.

Note the changes that occur in the tadpole. Compare the tadpole with the frog or toad.

For the study of the frog, follow a similar plan to the one given for the study of gnawers.

FOURTH YEAR.

INSECTS.

Study the paper wasp, the mud wasp, the caterpillar and butterfly, and the silkworm and silk moth.

Collections of insects studied should be made so that each child may have a specimen for investigation.

The spinning of the cocoons by the larvæ should be watched by the children and the time noted which elapses before the perfect insects appear.

The parts of each insect studied should be noted and the adaptation of parts to modes of living dwelled upon.

Secure, if possible, the nest of the paper wasp and the mud wasp.

Note peculiar habits of the insects studied, their weapons of defense, food, length of life, etc.

Likenesses and differences between the insects studied should be observed and conclusions drawn.

Children should write many descriptions and narrations of insects studied either from outlines or questions.

Many interesting stories about insects from standard authors should be read and reproduced by the children.

Short, appropriate poems about insects should be memorized by the children.

The insects studied should be drawn and appropriately colored.

MAMMALS.

Study the dog, the cat and the bear as types of the families they represent.

Work with the specimens before the children when practicable.

The study of the characteristic features of the animals considered, together with the adaptation of structure to use and to environment, should be a strong feature of the work.

The peculiar habits, food and how obtained, modes of defense, etc., of each animal should be noted.

Children should be directed to the Zoological Gardens and to the National Museum to discover other animals having similar characteristic parts to the type animals studied.

Comparisons between animals of the same family and also between animals of the different families studied, should be written by the children.

Descriptions of both type animals and of families should be written by the children either from outline or questions.

Appropriate descriptions and narrations about the animals studied from standard authors should be read and reproduced by the children.

Short, appropriate poems about the animals studied should be memorized by the children.

The animals studied, together with the characteristic parts of each, should be drawn by the children.

These drawings should be appropriately colored.

BIRDS.

Lead children to discover characteristic features which distinguish birds from other animals.

Obtain a skeleton of a bird to show structure, lightness of bones, etc.

Study the structure of the feathers of birds.

Note the arrangement of feathers on the bodies.

Study types of land birds, water birds and air birds.

Work with the specimens before the children.

From a study of likenesses and differences in structure and habits, establish the three groups—land, water and air birds.

Compare and contrast birds of the same group, as; the duck and grebe and establish the families Swimmers and Divers.

Observe likenesses and differences between birds of the other groups and draw conclusions.

Use the Zoological Gardens and the National Museum in this work.

Let the comparisons made furnish the subjects for written compositions.

Write many descriptions and narrations of birds either from outline or questions.

Children should read descriptions and stories of birds from standard authors for reproduction.

The birds studied and characteristic parts of each should be drawn, and each drawing appropriately colored.

Physiology.

FIRST YEAR.

The human body lessons in the first grade should be very general, covering the main features of the body and its care. The study affords an excellent opportunity for training the children in habits of order, neatness and propriety. From this it will be seen that the lessons on the care of the body should emphasize quite as much the *when* as the *how* of such care.

Language teaching should be carried on simultaneously with that of physiology and hygiene. The *expression* of what the child learns here is of as much importance as the *facts* he learns and is a good test of the definiteness, clearness, precision and completeness of his acquisition of those facts.

The course in physiology for the first year includes the study of the following :

I. Head
II. Trunk
III. Upper extremities
IV. Lower extremities
V. The skin—the general protection of the body against cold, dampness and uncleanliness

I. Head

Parts
- Top or crown
- Front or face
- Sides
- Back

1. The hair covering the front and back parts—use

Care
- Combing
- Brushing
- Keeping clean and neat

2. On the sides of the head are the ears. Their use—hearing

Care { Cleanse with warm water—how often?
Do not put objects into them.
Do not pick them with sharp instruments.

3 Front
- Forehead—position
- Eyes
  - Parts
  - Position of each part
  - Use of each part
  - Care of each part
  - Care { Keep clean; do not rub them; do not rub them when cinders get into them; do not strain them by looking at the sun; by using in poor light or looking cross-eyed. When reading, let the light fall over the left shoulder.
- Nose
  - Position
  - Uses
  - Care { Keep clean; proper time—manner; do not put substances into the nose.
- Cheeks—position, right and left
- Lips and use—upper and lower
- Chin—position

II. Trunk—general use—to hold together all parts of the body

III. Upper extremities

Parts { Arm
Fore-arm
Wrist
Hand

Give the position of each part.

Give the connection of parts—joints.
Give parts and positions of parts of hand—back, thumb, nails, palm, fingers.

Uses of hand
- Work (elaborate)
- Carrying food to mouth
- Protection

Care of hand
- Keep dry and clean.
- Keep the nails clean and short (when and how).
- Do not bite the nails.
- Do not strain the joints by pulling apart and making them crack.

IV. Lower extremities

Thigh, leg, ankle, foot
Position of each part
Connection of each part

Foot
- Parts—heel, instep, sole, toes
- Position—heel, instep, sole, toes
- Uses—running, walking, jumping
- Care
  - Keep clean.
  - Position when
    - Sitting
    - Standing
    - Walking
  - Do not stand on the side of the foot.
  - Avoid wearing tight shoes.

V. Skin
Use
Care
- Keep clean.
- Bathing—when, how often, how.

SECOND YEAR.

(See first year course).
The work this year should be more definite than it is possible or desirable to make it the first year.

The same general course given for the first year may be pursued, emphasizing the laws of health, and giving special attention to the evil effects of narcotics and intoxicants.

THIRD YEAR.

During the second half of the year, use the Child's Health Primer as a supplementary reading book to page 61. Supplement this book by conversational lessons, leading the pupils to talk freely and connectedly, giving especial emphasis to the evil effects of the use of narcotics and intoxicants.

Bones:

Make a collection of bones; observe form, size, color, covering, etc.

Classify: long, short, flat and irregular bones. Locate, give use, and note the adaptation of form or structure to use.

Peel off the membrane covering a fresh bone. Pound or grind a dry bone to powder.

Obtain, by sawing, tranverse and longitudinal sections of fresh bones and old dry bones.

Observe tissue, cells, marrow and openings for the entrance of blood vessels.

Steep a long bone in diluted nitric acid for a few days. Take it out, stretch it, bend it, tie it in a knot. Account for the change from a hard, unyielding, to a soft, pliable, elastic substance.

Burn a bone in an open fire for a short time. Strike it gently. Why does it break and crumble? Account for the change in substance. What has the bone lost?

Obtain a fresh joint from the market; observe the color and texture of the cartilage coat at the ends of the bones.

Cut a section of a joint; observe its working. Locate and give use of the principal joints of the body.

Muscle:

Procure some lean meat; call attention to the color, bundles of fibers and the connective tissue between and around the muscles.

Observe meat after it has been cooked in various ways ; also pressed beef and chipped beef.

Boil a piece of corned beef; tear into shreds the bundles of fibers, which separate easily, and observe under a microscope.

Any lean meat will serve as an example of a voluntary muscle while the heart or the coating of the stomach furnishes illustrations of an involuntary muscle.

Explain the action of each in regard to the will, and show that when a muscle shortens its length it increases in thickness.

FOURTH YEAR.

Complete the Child's Health Primer from page 60 as supplementary reading matter.

See Reading, fourth year.

The Heart:

Get a beef's heart from the market ; call attention to shape and color, and show by reference to the manikin the position of the heart in the human body, and how it is protected.

Notice the veins and arteries and give the use of each, by *briefly* tracing the circulation of the blood through the heart.

Listen to the beating of the heart, and feel the pulse in the wrist and neck.

Run or exercise in some way and observe the quickened action of the heart.

The Lungs:

Wash and carefully dry the lungs of a sheep. Observe number, shape, color, location and lobes.

Inflate the lungs by breathing through the trachea.

Cut a transverse section of the trachea.

Show how it is held open by rigid rings of cartilage. How are the rings completed in the back?

Cut away the lung tissue exposing the bronchi and bronchial tubes ; notice the air cells and the spongy, elastic substance of the lung tissue. Throw a piece in some water. Why does it float?

Obtain, if possible, the swimming bladder of a fish or the lungs of a reptile. Compare with the lungs of other animals.

The Skin:

Examine the pores of the skin with a microscope. Their use. Importance of keeping them open.

Teach briefly; the layers of the skin, number, color, composition, name and use; the tissues—connective and adipose—texture, distribution, location and use; the sweat glands and modifications of the skin, the hair and nails.

FIFTH YEAR.

Use Hygiene for Young People to page 109, for supplementary reading.

See Reading, fifth year.

The most effective way of teaching the evil results of the use of narcotics and intoxicants is to show the real nature of tissue and the ease with which it is destroyed or made incapable of performing its proper functions in sustaining life and giving enjoyment.

Bones:

Soak a bone in weak muriatic acid to remove the mineral matter. Its hardness and solidity gone, the bone may be bent and tied in a knot.

Subject a bone to strong heat to remove the animal matter. It is now very brittle and will break or crumble at the slightest touch.

Cut a section of a fresh bone and peel off the dense fibrous membrane on the exterior. What is its use? Notice the marrow.

Saw an old bone lengthwise and notice the loose, spongy interior with its communicating cells and spaces.

Obtain a joint from the market, remove the outer layer of tissue and observe the strong, compact ligaments.

Cut a fresh joint, notice the watery fluid which escapes from the membrane investing the cartilage. Its use.

Cut a longitudinal section of a joint to see how smoothly it works; observe also, the strength of the ligaments and the deep shining layers of cartilage.

Cut the cushion of cartilage between two adjoining vertebræ. Compare with the cartilage found at the joints.

Muscle:

Examine a piece of lean meat, noticing the bundles of delicate ruddy fibers and the whitish connective tissue.

Compare the solid voluntary muscles and the hollow involuntary muscles as to general appearance, distribution, numbers, use and domination by the will.

Procure the leg of a fowl for showing tendons and illustrating their use.

Show how a muscle in use shortens in length and increases in thickness. Explain "muscular contractility," and show the dependence of the body upon it for performing ordinary motions, as well as for changing the expression of the face in reflecting the emotions.

Digestive Organs:

Observe the digestive organs of a rabbit or a chicken. Though differing from those of the human body, they may be studied to advantage and comparisons drawn.

While not to be studied exhaustively, a general knowledge should be obtained of the machinery for dividing and grinding the food; of the fluids for dissolving it and of the canals and receptacles through which it passes.

Models which will be found helpful for the work of this grade may be seen at the Medical Museum.

SIXTH YEAR.

Hygiene for Young People completed from page 108.

The Respiratory Organs:

Procure from a butcher a complete larynx, an organ of respiration. Observe its shape, position, the epiglottis and vocal chords.

Obtain from the same source the lungs of an ox or a sheep; cleanse in cold water and dry carefully.

Cut a section of the trachea; observe the rigid rings of cartilage which prevent it from collapsing; the connective tissue binding the rings together and the membranous lining.

Inflate the lungs with a pair of bellows or breathe into the trachea through a tube, making them expand as in inspiration. They will collapse as in expiration as soon as the mouth or bellows is removed.

Cut away the spongy mass of lung tissue; observe the interior of the lungs, the bronchi and bronchial tubes and show by a microscope the air cells at the ends of the tubes.

Fill the lungs with air and throw them into a tub of water; they float. Exhaust the air; why do they shrivel and sink?

Give exercises in breathing to further illustrate inspiration and expiration.

The Heart:

Have the butcher furnish a heart enclosed in the pericardium or membranous sac. Rip the bag with a pair of scissors; notice the inner and outer layers of membrane. Which is attached to the heart? What is the use of the fluid which escapes from between the layers?

Cut the heart open to show the cavities.

Compare the upper and lower cavities.

Give reasons for differences.

Compare the right and left ventricle; observe the walls, partitions and linings. Find cause for the difference in size and structure by comparing the work performed by each.

Notice the aorta and the pulmonary artery.

Compare walls of veins and arteries.

Cut the ventricles away from the auricles so that the thin membranous valves between them may be exposed.

Illustrate by the manikin or models at the Medical Museum, the circulation of the blood through the body.

EIGHTH YEAR.

Steel's Hygienic Physiology. Have the chapters, "Circulation" and "Digestion of Food" read aloud in the class giving as much illustration and experiment as possible. This need not occupy more than four weeks.

"The Nervous System" and "The Special Senses" are the especial work of the grade. The collateral reading found in this book is all that need be attempted.

Nervous System and Special Senses:

The teacher of this grade is urged to visit the Medical Museum, where many specimens which can not be obtained for class use are carefully preserved.

Excellent models of the brain, ear, eye, etc., with full descriptive catalogue, may be obtained by responsible persons and studied to advantage.

The Brain:

Procure a calf's brain; notice form, color, size, weight, convolutions, fissures and lobes.

Cut a vertical section, exposing internal structure, the parts and their arrangement.

Cerebrum—Observe the hemispheres, the band of white nervous tissue connecting them, and the gray nerve substance forming the exterior of the hemisphere.

Cut a transverse section; observe internal structure, white nerve substance, etc.

Cerebellum—Observe location, hemispheres, parallel ridges and furrows. Compare with the cerebrum.

Cut a vertical section; observe the nerve substance of the interior and the arbor vitæ.

The medulla oblongata and pons Varolii may be studied respecting location, structure, color, etc., from a vertical section of the brain.

Obtain, if possible, the brain of one of the lower animals—a frog or a pigeon—for purposes of comparison.

(A brain may be preserved for several lessons by freezing it or by preserving it in alcohol.)

The Eye:

Procure from the market a calf's eye. Carefully dissect it, observing the coats, their number, texture, color; the vitreous humor; crystalline lens and the optic nerve or the place where it enters the ball.

Freeze an eye; cut a vertical section. The parts and their arrangement can perhaps be seen to better advantage.

Continue the study of the eye from the manikin or models which show the cavity, the muscles which hold it in place making motion possible.

Other Organs of Special Senses:

The ear and the nose can best be studied from large models; a beef's tongue will aid in the study of the tongue, while the skin should be tested on different parts of the body, to show varying degrees of delicacy and acuteness.

Physics.

SEVENTH YEAR.

SUGGESTIONS TO TEACHERS.

The purpose of the following experiments is not primarily to teach facts in physical science. It is to cultivate in the child a habit of exact observation, and a power to form correct inferences from the facts observed. To do this the mind of the child must be brought into direct contact with facts.

In the development of this work the pupil should make the experiments under the guidance of the teacher.

The pupils should prepare the apparatus, using always the most inexpensive material.

No set definitions need be learned.

Pupils should be made to talk connectedly, logically and correctly, describing what they do, telling what they observe, and stating their conclusions.

No notes need be taken by the pupils, and, of course, no definitions or conclusions recorded for memorizing.

From time to time formal compositions may be made by the children, the experiments, the observations and the conclusions, appertaining to and resulting from a single unit of work, affording the best possible outline for such composition.

Pupils should be encouraged to make experiments other than those suggested in this course.

Encourage the pupils at all times to know the common application of facts developed to the practical processes of life.

If the pupil is to learn *to see* and *to conclude*, the teacher must dictate nothing. Didactic teaching does not train the pupil in self activity, nor strengthen him in channels of original investigation and determining.

(See Teachers' Manual, pamphlet form.)

OUTLINE OF PHYSICS.

I. **Matter and its Properties:**

  a Impenetrability
  b Divisibility; the molecule
  c Porosity; the relative position of molecules
  d Density; the quantity of matter in given volumes
  e Phenomena of attraction; gravitation, cohesion, adhesion
      1 Gravitation—weight, center of gravity
      2 Cohesion—hardness, flexibility, elasticity, brittleness, malleability, etc.
      3 Adhesion—capillarity
  f Theory of the constitution of matter.
  g Three states of matter—solid, liquid, and gaseous.

II. **Mechanics:**

  a Solids
      1 Machines—lever, inclined plane, pulley; uses of machines
  b Fluids
      1 Liquids
         (a) Pressure—transmission of pressure; pressure due to gravity
         (b) Buoyancy—floating bodies
         (c) Equilibrium
      2 Gases—the atmosphere
         (a) Pressure—barometer, siphon, common pump.

III. **Heat:**

  a Sources of heat; ways of producing heat:
      1 By mechanical force
      2 By chemical force

b Effects of heat in matter:
:   1 Expansion and contraction — solids, liquids and gases; the thermometer
    2 Change of state: (a) liquefaction and solidification; (b) vaporization and liquefaction.
c Communication of heat:
:   1 Conduction—solids
    2 Convection—liquids and gases
    3 Radiation.

IV. Sound:

a Nature of sound—vibrations
b Transmission of sound—solids, liquids and gases.

Penmanship.

FIRST YEAR.

Use the cards and tablets provided for the grade ; copy on ruled paper phrases and sentences, taken from the children's compositions, and written by the teacher on the blackboard.

At an early day write the compositions, as entireties, made by the children.

Caution.—Do not tire the children with too much writing, which tends to discourage them and make them careless. Tired children can not do their best work.

Let the children always be kept to their best efforts. Show the children how to make correct letter and word forms. Let the children see these forms made on the board. Much blackboard work on the part of the teacher is profitable.

SECOND YEAR.

For the first eight weeks, without copy-books, thorough drill in position, pencil holding and movements. Practice small and capital letters. After this, with lead pencil, use copy-book No. 2.

The teacher should represent much work on the blackboard in the presence of the children.

All the written work of the children should be criticised as carefully as that done in the copy-book. While writing, lead the child to make his best effort.

Caution.—Study the work to be done and the condition of the child, and do not ask him to write when tired.

THIRD YEAR.

For the first eight weeks, without copy-book, thorough drill in pen-holding, position and movements; after this with pen and ink, use copy-book No. 3. The teacher can accomplish much good by showing the formation of letters and words on the blackboard. Much of this should be done.

FOURTH YEAR.

For the first eight weeks, without copy-book, thorough drill in position, pen-holding and movements. Review small and capital letters. Copy-book No. 4.

All written exercises should be carefully criticised by the teacher with respect to form, capitalization, punctuation and penmanship. Examine and criticise as a general exercise in the hearing of all the children. Do not let the children write after they become tired.

FIFTH YEAR.

For the first eight weeks, without copy-book, thorough drill in position, pen-holding and movements. Review small and capital letters. Copy-book No. 5.

Examine and criticise note books, arithmetical analyses, etc., etc. Allow no careless work in form or in penmanship.

SIXTH YEAR.

For the first eight weeks, without copy-book, thorough drill in position, pen-holding and movements. Review small and capital letters. Copy-book No. 7.

Make every reasonable effort to secure careful work in all written exercises. The position of the pupil should be criticised when doing any written work.

SEVENTH YEAR.

For the first eight weeks, without copy-book, thorough drill in position, pen-holding and movements. Review small and capital letters. Copy-book No. 8.

All written work of the grade should be inspected and criticised. The pupil should not be allowed to do any written work carelessly.

EIGHTH YEAR.

For the first eight weeks, without copy-book, thorough drill in position, pen-holding and movements. Review small and capital letters. Copy-book No. 8 for boys; No. 10 for girls.

The form and penmanship of work in note-books and written analyses, and other exercises, should be criticised to secure neatness and legibility in all written work.

Drawing.

FIRST YEAR.
SEPTEMBER, OCTOBER, NOVEMBER, DECEMBER.

Two hours per week; daily lessons.
Materials—Clay, paper, pencil, models, colored paper.

Drill*
- Position
  - in modeling
  - in drawing
- Movement
  - from left to right
  - forward and backward
  - circular
- Use of pencil
  - vertical lines
  - horizontal lines
  - circles

Modeling in clay†
- Geometric solids
  - sphere
  - hemisphere
  - cube
  - cylinder
  - square prism
  - right-angled triangular prism
- Objects based on geometric forms
  - apple
  - peach
  - orange
  - grapes
  - tomato
  - onion
  - nuts
  - sugar bowl
  - teapot
  - ginger jar
  - bowl
  - hat
  - cap
  - box
  - square inkstand
  - toy house
  - rolling pin
  - mallet
  - bottle

*See Appendix A.
† See Appendix B.

Color { Study of spectrum { Present spectrum, using a glass prism. Cut oblongs of all the colors of the spectrum 2x¾ inch.

Language { The right use in sentences of terms pertaining to the posiions and forms of the objects modeled { right / left / on / under / middle / centre / sphere / circle / roll / stand / cube / face / corner / edge / smaller / larger / round / square / flat / cylinder, oblong, hemisphere.

The Purposes of this Unit of Work are:

1. To develop by cumulative effort, true conceptions of the geometric solids.

2. To lead the children to see these forms as the bases of many familiar forms.

3. To lead them to see in these solids the details of surfaces, edges and corners.

4. To train them in giving correct oral expression to the ideas thus acquired.

5. To give strength and flexibility to the muscles of the hand and arm.

6. To form the habit of maintaining a healthful position of the body.

7. To awaken the inventive ability.

8. To cultivate true ideas of beauty in form, color and arrangement.

REMARKS.

To accomplish the ends enumerated above, make free use of the models provided for the children. While studying the solids bring into the school-room objects based on them. Let the children select from their groups of models the solid suggested by each object.

Before modeling the geometric solids, study the models not only through the eye, but by handling them with closed eyes.

The children should criticise the clay forms modeled in a corresponding way.

Give much practice in arranging the solids in groups letting the children decide which is the most pleasing group. This should be done especially in developing ideas of position, as, also for the language work.

Develop the idea of planes by using tablets in connection with the solids. The edges of planes that are bounded by straight lines will be taught more easily by the use of the sticks in connection with the tablets.

When using the type forms do not allow the children to lose sight of their representation in other objects; the study of every geometric form should be supplemented by a careful study of the forms based on or derived from it.

In the color work given for this period do not teach the names of colors.

Lead the children to observe the rainbow colors refracted by a triangular prism of glass. Soap bubbles, the iridescence of pearl shells and iridescent glass, the neck of the peacock, and of the dove, will give conceptions of pure color and impress the lesson on the mind of the child.

After the colors are cut put them in envelopes for future use. Lead the children to see that in the prism and rainbow there is an order in the arrangement, that those colors nearest related are found together. Without the aid of the chart let the children try to discover some of these relations.

Note the results of these attempts, and record them for future reference. Do not correct the children.

TWO MONTHS—JANUARY AND FEBRUARY.

Time—two hours per week.
Materials—Colored sticks, one to five inches in length; paper, pencil, colored paper.

Drill exercises
- Lines limited in length
  - vertical lines
  - horizontal lines
  - oblique lines

*Tablet and Stick-laying
- Positions of lines
  - vertical
  - horizontal
  - oblique
- Divisions of lines—halves and fourths
- Combinations of lines in geometric figures
  - square
  - oblong rectangle
  - triangle
- Borders
  - arrangement of sticks in groups of vertical, horizontal and oblique lines
  - Greek fret
  - zigzag
  - repetition of tablets
- Invention
  - borders
  - other ornamental arrangements with sticks and tablets
- Letters—L, E, F, H, I, T.

Drawing
- Forms constructed with sticks
  - geometric forms, dictated arrangements and judicious selection from the children's inventions

Color
- Selections from spectrum colors
  - standard red
  - standard yellow
  - standard blue
  - related colors

---

*See Appendix C.

The Special Purposes of this Work are:

To lead the children to observe and to represent edges as the outlines of form.

To develop the ability to invent.

To train the fingers in care, accuracy and refinement in handling material.

To train the color sense.

To give the color lesson:
1. Show standard yellow, and let the children select from their groups of colored papers the corresponding color.
2. Bring samples of cloth, ribbon or worsted of this color, compare them with the colored papers.
3. Find in these groups of colors the nearest related color on each side of the selected color.

See if any of the specimens resemble this in color.

Arrange a group of three, taking yellow and finding the nearest related colors.

Take red in a corresponding way.

Do not use names until the close of this unit of work.

MARCH, APRIL, MAY, JUNE.

Time—Two hours per week.

Materials—Colored paper, pencil, paper, mucilage.

Drill { Lines vertical, horizontal and oblique { long lines / lines limited in length to three, four inches

Paper* Folding and Mounting
- Geometric planes { square with diameters and diagonals / oblong rectangle / right-angled triangle
- Divisions and combinations { square of two tints / Greek cross / border of squares / oblongs around a center / border of oblongs / border of triangles
- Invention { borders / arrangements around a centre

*See Appendix **D.**

- **Drawing**
  - The constructed paper forms
    - all geometric forms and dictated combinations
    - a judicious selection from the children's inventions
  - Objects
    - picture frames
    - flags
    - banners
    - school bags
    - pocket book
    - folded napkins or handkerchiefs
    - fans
    - picture cords
  - Plant forms
    - such forms as are studied in the course of the lessons on plants

- **Language**
  - Additional vocabulary used in these lessons
    - diameter
    - diagonal
    - space
    - front
    - back
    - tint
    - light
    - lighter

- **Color**
  - Recognition and names of the standard yellow, red and blue, with their tints
    - in the spectrum
    - in paper as it is used for folding
    - in flowers

- Water color painting, (optional)
  - folded geometric paper forms
  - flowers

The Special Purposes of this Work are:

To lead the children to see surface in the forms they make.

To train the color sense.

To cultivate an appreciation of harmonious combinations in both forms and colors.

To cultivate habits of neatness and accuracy in the use of materials.

The training in color at this period should be kept in close connection with the paper folding and with the study of plant forms. Children should observe carefully the colors of flowers, distinguishing the several tints. The spring flowers with which they are provided at this season are especially good for this exercise. When as in the violet they discover for themselves that the color does not match any of the tints of the colors they are using in the folding paper they should be led to look for a closer resemblance in the spectrum colors, but in all such exercises the teachers must remember that they are training the color sense and are not teaching merely the names of colors.

If expression is to be given by the use of water color:
1. Teach the handling of the brush and the management of the materials.
2. Let the children wash in tints imitating in forms and colors the geometric forms they are folding.
3. Let them try to imitate the forms and colors of some of the flowers they are handling, as the bluet and the buttercup.

SECOND YEAR.

SEPTEMBER, OCTOBER, NOVEMBER, DECEMBER.

Time—Two hours per week, daily lessons.
Materials—Clay, pencil, paper, models, colored paper.

Drill Exercises *
- Position
  - in moulding
  - in drawing
- Movement
  - from left to right
  - forward and backward
  - circular
- Use of pencil
  - vertical lines
  - horizontal lines
  - circles

---
*See Appendix A.

Modeling *
- Geometric solids
  - review of solids modeled in first year
  - ellipsoid
  - ovoid
  - equilateral triangular prism
  - cone
  - square pyramid
- Forms based on geometric solids
  - apples
  - plums
  - potatoes
  - bananas
  - lemons
  - pears
  - acorns
  - bottles
  - books
  - cups
  - bowls
  - vases
  - nests with eggs
- From memory
  - monument
  - chimney
  - roof

Color { Review of first year's work { with the spectrum colors by observation in nature

Language { The right use in sentences of terms pertaining to the forms of the objects modeled and to their positions in groups { Review with models first year vocabulary. ellipsoid ovoid, yellow, red, blue surface plane

The Purposes of this Unit of Work are:

1. To develop in the minds of the children a true conception of the geometric solids.

2. To lead them to see these forms as the bases of many familiar forms.

3. To lead them to see in these solids the details of surfaces, edges and corners.

---
* See Appendix B.

4. To train them in giving correct oral expression to the ideas thus acquired.
5. To give strength and flexibility to the muscles of the hand and arm preparatory to drawing.
6. To form the habit of maintaining a healthful position of the body.
7. To awaken the inventive ability.
8. To cultivate true ideas of beauty in form, color and arrangement (composition).

REMARKS.

To accomplish the purposes enumerated above make free use of the models provided. While studying the solids bring into the school-room familiar forms; let the children select from their groups of solids the one suggested by each object

Before modeling the geometric solids study the models not only through the eye but by handling them with closed eyes.

The children should criticise the clay forms modeled by them in a corresponding way. Let the children arrange the solids in groups (composition), after which let them learn to criticise such groupings or compositions. This should be done especially to develop true ideas of position as well as for the language work.

Develop the idea of planes by using the tablets in connection with the solids. In planes bounded by straight lines the idea of edges is more easily taught by the use of the sticks in connection with the tablets.

In using the type forms do not allow the children to lose sight of their connection with other objects; the study of a geometric form should be supplemented by the study of the forms based upon it.

In the color work given for this period the children having received training in the recognition of certain colors and tints, the names designating these sensations may be used. If good work in the training of the color sense is to be done throughout the year, the teacher must know that the children see the relations of the colors. For example they must see that orange is related to both red and yellow and must be able to recognize these colors in other places and connected with other materials before the entire class is taught to designate a particular spot in the spectrum by a given name.

JANUARY AND FEBRUARY.

Time—Two hours per week.

Materials—Colored sticks one to four inches in length, tablets, pencil, colored paper.

Drill Exercises { Use of pencil { vertical lines / horizontal lines / oblique lines

Tablet and stick laying*
- Short review of the first year's course
  - position of lines
  - square
  - rectangular oblong
  - triangles
- Parallel lines and angles
  - right angles
  - acute angles
  - obtuse angles
- Division of lines
  - halves
  - thirds
  - fourths
- Geometric forms
  - rhomb
  - rhomboid
  - trapezoid
  - equilateral triangle
  - isosceles triangle
  - right angle triangle
  - ellipse
  - oval
- Ornamental combinations
  - borders
  - stars
  - crosses
- Letters—A, V, K, N, M, W, X, Y.

---

* See Appendix C.

Drawing	Representation of forms constructed	From objects	fans envelopes slate paper cap side of book
		From memory	side of street lamp fences fans side of chimney monument
Language	Additional vocabulary required to describe these forms		angle right angle acute angle obtuse angle parallel rhomb rhomboid trapezoid equilateral isosceles star cross
Color	Selection from spectrum		orange green violet
	Relations of these colors to yellow, blue, red Groups of five		

Special Purposes of the Work are:

To lead the children to observe, and to represent edges as the outlines of form.

To develop the ability to invent.

To train the fingers to the careful handling required when constructing with sticks.

To train the color sense.

REMARKS.

To Give the Color Lesson:

1. Children select from their groups of colors the standard orange, the teacher pointing to the color on the chart.
2. Children find this color in the spectrum.
3. Children discover its relation to yellow and red by its position in the spectrum.
4. Children arrange this group (red, red orange, orange, yellow orange, yellow) with papers on the desk.
5. Teacher shows by experiment with water colors or other material how this color may be produced by uniting the red and yellow.
6. Children bring samples of cloth, ribbons or worsted.
7. They should see whether or not their samples match either paper. They will see perhaps that some of these samples have more red, some more yellow than the standard; let them look for similar colors in the spectrum.

Take green and violet in a corresponding way.

MARCH, APRIL, MAY, JUNE.

Time—two hours per week.
Materials—colored paper, pencil, paper, mucilage.

Drill
- Lines, vertical, horizontal and oblique
  - long lines
  - lines limited in length to three, four and five inches

Paper folding and mounting
- Geometric forms
  - trapezoid
  - isosceles triangle
  - right angle triangle
  - scalene triangle
  - rhomboid
  - rhombus
  - irregular pentagon
- Combinations dictated by the teachers and invented by the children
  - ornamental forms.
  - around a centre
  - borders

Drawing	The constructed paper forms	all geometric forms and dictated combinations / a judicious selection from the children's inventions
	Objects	folded paper caps / toy boats / shoe / kite
	From memory	side of church steeple
	Plant forms	such as are studied in the course of lessons for composition

Color	Tints and hues of orange, green, violet	in paper / in leaves and flowers / in geometric paper forms folded.

Water color painting (optional) { flowers and leaves

Special Purposes of this Work are:

To lead the children to see surfaces in the forms they make.
To train the color sense.
To cultivate an appreciation of harmonious combinations of both form and color.
To cultivate habits of neatness and accuracy in the use of materials.

The work in color should be kept in close connection with the paper folding and with the study of plant forms. The tints should first be studied by use of paper. Children should look for flowers having tints and hues of orange and violet and compare them with the tints of their papers and with the spectrum colors. They will find material for similar observation of the greens in the study of leaves.

If it is possible to use the water colors in representing the folded paper forms and the flowers and leaves, great interest will be added to the work as the representation of surface will be more complete.

THIRD YEAR.

SEPTEMBER, OCTOBER, NOVEMBER, DECEMBER.

Time—two hours per week.
Materials—pencil, paper, clay, slate or board.

- Drill exercises
  - Straight lines
    - vertical
    - horizontal
    - oblique
  - Curves
    - circles

- Modeling *
  - Geometric solids
    - sphere
    - cylinder
    - square prism
    - hemisphere
    - right-angled triangular prism
  - Objects based on geometric solids
    - bottles of various forms and proportions
    - vases and other pottery
    - potatoes
    - apples
    - nuts
    - gourds and other available objects

- Drawing
  - Different views of the solids moulded
    - front and top view of horizontal and vertical cylinder
    - front and top view of oblong rectangular prism
    - edge view of oblong and circular planes

- Color
  - Study of spectrum colors
    - related colors
    - Arrange spectrum colors without chart.

*See Appendix B, Part I.

Language { All terms involved in descriptions of the geometric forms and their correct application } { straight, curved, horizontal, oblique, vertical, sphere, circle, hemisphere, semi-circle, right angle, triangle, square, oblong, width, heighth, larger, smaller }

Purposes of this Unit of Work are:

1. To form the habit of maintaining a healthful position of the body.
2. To give strength and flexibility to the fingers, wrist and arms.
3. To give freedom, precision and lightness in the use of the pencil.
4. To develop true conceptions of form and color.
5. To give power to describe forms in correct language.
6. To give power to express with the pencil lines that describe contour.

In studying a form the order should be :
1. Observing by seeing and handling the model
2. Construction of the form in clay
3. Using and learning terms in descriptions

Children should be given every opportunity possible for handling the forms. Those children especially should handle the models who do not seem to get true conceptions readily through the eye.

Describing the forms by motions of the hand in the air is

helpful. It will be found helpful to have forms drawn on the board by a portion of the class, while the others criticise the work, comparing with the models.

The children should be trained from the beginning to make broad, grey lines. Children should learn early to criticise lines.

The lead of the pencil should be round, not pointed. The drawing pencil should not be used for any other purpose. Short pencils should not be used for any purpose.

Children should be trained to hold the pencil two inches from its point.

To give the color lesson children may cut oblongs representing all the spectrum colors each having the proportion of ½ inch x 2 inches; put the oblongs in envelopes.

1. Let the children select the standard orange and place on each side the nearest related color.
2. Treat the standard green in the same way.
3. Treat the standard violet in the same way.
4. Let the children place the remaining colors.
5. Let the children unite the groups.

Continue exercises of this kind until the children can lay the spectrum without assistance.

JANUARY AND FEBRUARY.

Time—two hours per week.
Materials—pencil, paper, objects.

Drill Exercises		
	Straight lines	limited in length from 2 to 6 inches / united to form angles
	Circles	of given size
	Curves	quadrants, semi-circles

Object drawing
- Forms previously moulded
  - bottles
  - vases based on sphere
  - bowls
  - potatoes
  - apples
  - gourds
  - lemons
- Front views of flat forms
  - fans of different shapes
  - envelopes
  - wheels
  - United States shield
  - school bag and other available forms of similar character

Color
- Complementary colors
  - yellow
  - red
  - blue
  - orange
  - green
  - purple

Language
- Constant use of the vocabulary acquired in the first three months

The Purposes of this Unit of Work are:

To give drill in the continuous and direct application of the knowledge of forms obtained by observing and making during the first three months of the year and of the skill acquired in handling the pencil by drawing familiar objects, size and proportion being considered and emphasized.

To continue the training of the color sense.

In representing familiar objects the lesson may sometimes be given by the use of one or two large objects, but whenever it is possible it should be given by the use of many small objects, one object being found on each child's desk. Exact proportions should not be given. The objects should be studied as based on geometric forms of different proportions.

In representing fruits there should be at least one specimen for every three children. When each child has a model on his desk it should be placed near the level of the eye.

Before giving a pencil drill, one or more of the pupils should illustrate on the board for the class the correct method of holding the pencil, showing at the same time the order in which the lines should occur in combinations.

After illustration and direction, the lines and positions required, should be kept in the mind of the pupil to be executed in order in response to signals, one for each line.

For the Color Lesson:

Lay complementary colors, taking yellow, red and blue, and selecting the complementary or contrasting colors.

MARCH, APRIL, MAY, JUNE.

Material—colored paper, pencil, paper, scissors, rubber eraser.

Paper folding and cutting*
- Studying of superimposed tints
  - cutting and pasting rosettes
- Modifications of units
  - modifications by straight lines and curves
  - modifications of proportions to fill spaces
- Arrangement in geometric form
  - square
  - rectangular oblong
  - rhomb
  - triangle
  - borders

Drawing
- From the paper forms { units and arrangements
- From nature { leaves

*See Appendix D, Part II.

Water Color Painting, optional:

Materials—colors, brushes, water-color paper

Flat washes
- Tints of primaries { in oblong 3x6
- Coloring of decorative arrangements in the 3 tints of primaries { arrangements around a centre and borders

Language
- Additional form vocabulary { units, symmetry, symmetrical balance
- Additional color vocabulary { tints, light, lighter

The Special Purposes of this Unit of Work are:

To cultivate a correct taste for the beautiful in form and color.

To awaken the desire of the pupil to express by the work of his own hands the order, grace and fitness shown in nature and in good art.

To teach such of the underlying principles of beauty as he is capable of understanding; to develop the inventive faculty.

To give him right terms to express in words his ideas.

To train him in the use of pencil, paper, scissors and adhesive materials.

The results of the drill exercises should be evident in all that the children do at this time. They should sit well, hold the pencil correctly, and draw lines with freedom. The teacher will need to watch these points with care.

When the lesson involves drawing, it is wise to precede it by a short concert drill.

For the Color Lesson there should be:

1. Recognition by matching of colors used in folding, and their tints.

2. Recognition of their composition and of the predominating color in each. This should be done in connection with the paper folding and cutting.

3. Matching in other materials as cloth, silk, ribbon, worsted.

FOURTH YEAR.

SEPTEMBER, OCTOBER, NOVEMBER, DECEMBER.

Time—Three hours per week.
Materials—Pencil, paper, clay, slate or board.

Drill Exercises
- Straight lines combined in geometric forms
  - triangles
  - squares
  - rectangles
- Curves
  - circle
  - ellipse
  - oval

Modeling*
- Geometric solids
  - sphere
  - ellipsoid
  - ovoid
  - triangular prism
  - cone
  - square pyramid
- Objects based on these geometric solids
  - vases
  - pitchers
  - bottles and other available pottery forms
- Fruits and vegetables
  - pear
  - melon
  - squash
  - banana
  - carrot
  - beet
  - acorn and other available forms
- Modeling to definite proportions
  - a cube, 2½ inches

Drawing
- Different views of geometric forms.

---
*See Appendix B, Part I.

Color*	Review of third grade course.	laying spectrum from memory colors and tints recognition of tints in material
Language	All terms involved in descriptions of the geometric forms and their correct application	straight curved vertical horizontal oblique ellipse, ellipsoid circle sphere oval, ovoid angle triangle acute right obtuse equilateral isosceles

Purposes of this Unit of Work are:

To cultivate the habit of assuming a healthful position when at work.

To give strength and flexibility to the fingers, wrist and arm.

To lead the pupil to recognize resemblance, and lesser differences of contour and proportions.

To train the pupil to describe the forms, using the necessary terms intelligently.

To give him power to express with the pencil as accurately as possible, the lines that give the contour of the geometric form.

To continue the training of the color sense.

In presenting a new form let the order of development be:

1. Observation by comparing with other forms, seeing and handling the form.

---
*See Color, Third Grade.

2. Making in clay.
3. Terms and oral description.

If there are children who seem to get no conception of form through the eye, endeavor to give them more opportunities of handling the objects. Describing the form in the air is helpful, as are also trials at making them on the blackboard.

JANUARY AND FEBRUARY.

Materials—pencil, paper, rubber eraser.

Drill Exercises	Straight lines combined in geometric forms	rectangles, triangles
	Curves	circular, oval curves, simple and reversed
Object Drawing	Upright views of forms previously moulded	vases, pitchers and other pottery forms
	Study of the appearance of the circle in various positions	cylinder, cylindrical objects
	Study of the appearance of squares and oblong planes	cube, oblong block
	Groups of fruit and vegetables	apples, pears, lemons, oranges, squash, potatoes, bananas, etc
Language	Constant use of the vocabulary acquired in the first three months in describing form	Special attention to correct use of terms expressing dimensions and proportions as large, long, wide, high, small, etc

Color { Shades and tints of color. Scale of tones.

There should be a special effort on the part of the teacher to impress upon the mind of the pupil that he is to draw his own view of the object and not a preconceived idea.

The objects should not be elaborate in form or ornamentation. No change of view should be permitted before the drawing is completed.

The children should be taught to place their drawings properly on the paper, and to make the size conform to the space. Give special attention to the use of the terms; longer, larger, smaller, wider, narrower, proportion, size.

· For the color lessons distribute papers of any color.
1. Children hold color toward the light, then away from the light, and note difference; see the cause of the difference. Teach difference between shade and tint.
2. Distribute shades and tints of color, lay scale of tones.
3. Give and define the term—tone.
4. Paste scales.

MARCH, APRIL, MAY, JUNE.

Materials—Colored paper, pencil, scissors, glue or mucilage, rubber, eraser, paper.

Paper folding and cutting
- Study of superimposed tints
  - tints and shades
  - cutting and pasting rosettes
- Modification of units
  - by curves derived from the study of leaf forms in proportions to fill spaces
- Arrangement in geometric forms
  - circle
  - pentagon
  - hexagon
  - octagon
  - borders

Drawing	From the paper form	units and arrangements	
	From nature	leaves	
Color	Values	arrangement of oblongs cut from paper to show the relative values of the primary and secondary colors	
	Complementary colors.	Cut square of secondary color, mount upon it small circle of the complementary primary.	

Water Color Painting, Optional:

Materials—Colors, brush, water-color paper.

Washes	Tints of secondaries and tertiaries	in oblongs 3x6
	Color scales of primaries and secondaries	
	One set of oblongs giving values Coloring decorative arrangements in two or three tints of secondaries.	arrangements around a centre borders

The Special Purposes of this Unit of Work are:

To cultivate a correct taste for the beautiful in form and color; to awaken the desire of the pupil to express in the work of his own hands the order, grace and fitness shown in nature and in good art.

To teach such of the underlying principles of beauty as he is capable of understanding; to develop the inventive faculty.

To give him right terms to express in words his ideas.

To train him in the use of material, pencil, paper, scissors, and adhesive materials.

The results of the drill exercises should be evident in all that the children do at this time. They should sit well, hold the pencil correctly and draw lines with freedom. The teacher will need to watch these points with care.

It is wise to precede a drawing exercise by a concert drill three minutes long.

Color lessons are to be given in connection with paper cutting and design.

1. Cut rosettes of tints, half the class with normal color on the outside, half with lightest tint on the outside.
2. Cut rosettes of shades, half with darkest shades on the outside, half with normal color on the outside.
3. Cut rosettes of tints and shades, half the class with darkest shade on the outside, half with lightest tints on the outside, each half using a different color. A language lesson may be given and a composition developed with these rosettes giving names of colors and terms used in connection with tints and shades.

FIFTH YEAR.

SEPTEMBER, OCTOBER, NOVEMBER, DECEMBER.

Time—Three hours per week.
Materials—Clay, model paper, mucilage, pencil, practice paper, models, ruler with parts of inches marked and having metal edge.

Drill Exercises. { Geometric plans { square, rectangles, triangles, circle

Construction	Modeling a solid to definite proportions	cylinder and cone 4x2. Cut cylinder for review on rectangular, oblong, semicircle, quadrant; cut cones for circle, ellipse, isosceles triangle, right angled triangle.
	Working-drawings	cube plane of paper cylinder oblong prism boxes-square, circular, oblong, triangle, cone and square pyramid
	Development of pattern from working-drawing and making paper model	cube square prism
Color	Study of spectrum colors	laying spectrum from memory selection from spectrum recognizing and naming colors and tints
Language	Special attention to be given to the use of words used in the description of surfaces and solids, and to the conventions of working drawings	dimension length breadth thicknesss height width centre lines working lines

The Purposes of this Unit of Work are:

To give the pupils an idea of one of the uses to which drawing is applied in industrial pursuits.

To teach them to make working-drawings and patterns of a few simple geometric solids and to show them how they can apply this knowledge in making some useful objects.

To give them power to make these working-drawings with a free hand.

To train them to neatness and accuracy in the use of the materials.

SUGGESTIONS.

The drill on the geometric planes should be preceded by a careful study of lengths in inches on the ruler. The ruler should then be put in the desk and the attention of the children called to the proportions of the figure, the order in which the lines are to be drawn and the changes in the positions of the hand.

The entire figure should then be drawn by count to keep the class together. Do not give directions line by line. The children should be strong enough to carry in mind a conception of the entire form and the order in which the work is to be done.

In developing the idea of the pattern a sketch of it should be made free-hand. In drawing the pattern for making the form it should be carefully ruled and measured. The right use of the ruler, the best method of laying out the work, economy of material and neatness in putting the parts of the pattern together should be attended to in this exercise.

Great care should be taken that words are used correctly in all conversations connected with the subject of working-drawings.

JANUARY, FEBRUARY, MARCH.

Materials—Model paper, mucilage, practice paper, ruler with parts of inches marked, and having metal edges.

Construction	Working drawings	block or brick of three dimensions steps—cross equilateral triangular prism spool tumbler book	
	Development of pattern from working drawings and making paper models	triangular prism boxes square and oblong	
Drill Exercises	Ellipses	horizontal of different widths	
Object Drawing	Study of the appearance of the circle	horizontal and level with the eye above and below the eye	
	Study of the appearance of other planes		
	Appearance of cylinder Appearance of cube Appearance of cone	upright in front of and above and below the level of the eye	
	Appearance of tumbler		
	Appearance of tin bucket and other cylinderical forms		
Color	Neutral gray and and brown and their tints Harmony of standard colors with neutrals		

The Purposes of this Work are:

To continue the work of the first part of the year in construction.

To call the attention of the children to the differences between the facts of form and their appearances as illustrated by working drawings and pictures.

To train the children to see the appearances.

To teach them to represent the appearances of a few simple forms, the facts of which they have already observed and represented.

APRIL, MAY, JUNE.

Material—Pencil, paper, colored paper, clay.

Drill Exercises
- Curves
  - elliptical
  - oval
  - reversed

Water color, optional
- Graded washes
  - primary and secondary colors
- Borders and rosettes
  - in tints of neutral gray and brown

Decorations
- Modeling leaves from nature
  - ivy
  - magnolia
- Carving in clay or other materials
  - lotus
  - rosette
- Drawing from nature
  - leaves
- Adaptation of natural leaf to ornament
  - rosettes
  - borders
- Applications of designs
  - decorating a box with paper cutting
  - doilies embroidered in outline stitch
  - tiles modeled or carved in clay

The Purposes of this Work are:

To lead the pupils to observe the beauty of subtle curves, and the harmony of color in ornament and in nature.

To awaken the desire to reproduce this beauty in their own work.

To train their hands to precision and freedom of movement in the drawing and modeling of these curves.

To teach them that designs for ornament must be adapted to space, and to the material used.

SUGGESTIONS.

It is desirable that each child should make an application of his work in decoration to some material that he can handle.

The materials suggested are those most easily procured, but pupils need not be limited to the use of these. The designs should be made in the school-room, and criticised by the teacher.

SIXTH YEAR.

SEPTEMBER, OCTOBER, NOVEMBER, DECEMBER.

Time—Three hours per week.

Materials—Model paper, mucilage, pencil, practice paper, eraser, compass, models, ruler with parts of inches marked and having metal edge.

Construction
- Review of principles of construction
  - cone
  - cylinder
  - rectangular solid
- Drill in geometric forms
  - square
  - rectangles of different proportions
  - triangles
- Free-hand working drawings
  - square prism with plinth
  - square pyramid
  - timber cut for joining
  - hexagonal prism
  - hammer or mallet
  - other common objects
- Development of pattern from working drawings and making paper model
  - square prism
  - sqare plinth
  - square pyramid
  - hexagonal prism
  - cone
  - cylinder

All that is said in connection with the course for the fifth year applies to the work of this year. The additional subjects taken, the representation of the invisible parts of solids, foreshortening, working-drawings for objects that are not to be made in paper. This last exercise should be individual work from objects in the hands of the children.

Children should be encouraged to make working-drawings and from these to construct objects in different kinds of materials. No exact directions can be given for this as the same materials may not be accessible to all. Wood, tin, clay, fullers earth and cardboard are some of the materials most easily procured. These objects should not be made in the school room. The work should be suggested, guided and encouraged, but not required. No object should be approved or exhibited that does not conform to a working-drawing.

JANUARY, FEBRUARY, MARCH.

Materials—Paper, pencil, eraser.

Perspective representation	Foreshortening of planes	rectangular curve
	Appearance of objects in front of and below the level of the eye	cylinder square plinth books
	Concentric circles	boxes bowls cylinder with square plinth
	Groups	three geometric solids three objects, a box or a book, combined with a vase, a tumbler or some similar form and some object based on the sphere, ellipsoid or ovoid
Decoration	Drill on symmetrical curves	from Moorish ornaments from Fleur-de-lis
	Modification of bilateral units	change of outline change of proportion addition of details
	Use of bilateral units	surface of designs

The Purposes of this Unit of Work are:

To lead the pupils to observe the changes in the appearances of forms produced by a change of position.

To teach them to reproduce this appearance in drawings of familiar forms.

To lead them to see and to draw a group of forms as a whole.

To lead them to see the beauty of symmetry in objects and in ornament.

To lead them to see the proper relations of subordinate units.

To teach them how units may be modified in contour, proportion and detail.

APRIL, MAY, JUNE.

Materials—Clay, paper, pencil.

Decoration
- Drawing from nature
  - opposite branching, two or three leaves
  - two or three leaves, radical
- Conventional bilateral arrangement
  - modification of units by curves derived from natural leaves
  - law of arrangement derived from natural growth
- Study and drawing of the top views of flowers
  - natural form
  - conventional form
- Modeling a plinth from a working-drawing
- Application to surface designs
  - conventionalized flower forms
- Modeling from nature
  - single leaf
  - branch of two leaves
- Cutting in clay or other material
  - Moorish ornament
- Application of design
  - Construct a box based on any geometric form.
  - Ornament it with a bilateral or surface design.
  - Draw its appearance in front of and below the level of the eye.

The Special Purposes of this Work are:

To awaken interest in the study of nature from an artistic stand-point.

To call attention to the laws of growth as illustrated in the branching of trees and in radical growth.

To lead the pupils to discover the bilateral growth in some natural forms.

To show them the uses made of this law of growth in art both in construction and ornament.

SEVENTH YEAR.

SEPTEMBER, OCTOBER, NOVEMBER, DECEMBER.

Time—Three hours per week.

Materials—Model paper, mucilage, two pencils, medium and hard, compasses, practice paper, ruler with parts of inches marked and having metal edge.

Free-hand Construction
- Working-drawing
  - rectangular block
  - chamfered block
  - moulding
  - bracket
  - halved together T joint

Instrumental Construction
- Use of compasses
  - circles
  - problems 1 and 2
  - applications
- Use of instruments and problems in making working drawings and patterns
  - washer
  - halved together T joint (dove-tailing)
  - cone
  - lamp shade
  - through mortise and tenon T joint
  - square frame
- Model making
  - cube*
  - square prism*
  - square plinth*
  - steps
  - cone
  - cylinder*
  - circular plinth*
  - lamp shade
- Read working drawings
  - Plans and elevations of objects with which the pupil is familiar

---

*Pupils may be excused from making these models in paper if not needed for object-drawing.

Pupils of this grade are expected to do accurate work, especially in construction.

They should be led to consider the use of instruments as an aid to the desired result.

Careless work should not be tolerated.

In problems, in working-drawings and in the making of the models the demand should be for results as near perfection as is possible with the means at command.

Many are entering the shops where accurate work with tools is required. The work here given is in harmony with these pursuits and trains the powers essential to success. Some of the working-drawings made will be used in the shops; some of these it will be observed are classed as free hand and some as instrumental. The advantages of each method should be recognized.

The pupils should be given many exercises in the reading of working-drawings. They should be led to realize the complete form of the solid represented and to describe it in correct language.

The first subjects taken for this exercise may be working-drawings of blocks of wood of different proportions with projections and incisions of various sizes, shapes and locations. Other objects should be selected with whose general characteristics the pupil is familiar.

Teachers who are unaccustomed to the reading of working-drawings will need to exercise great care in the selection and study of these drawings.

Precision in the use of language will be developed in geometrical definitions, in the wording of problems and in the reading of working-drawings.

Pupils may make of other materials than paper geometric solids and other objects. These should not be approved or exhibited as a part of the school work unless they conform to working-drawings made by the pupils. The material selected should so far as possible be adapted to the use of the object. Wood, clay, tin and cardboard are the most available materials. This work should be suggested and encouraged but not required.

JANUARY, FEBRUARY, MARCH.

Materials—Pencil, paper, eraser, models.

Perspective representation
- Review of the appearance of circles
  - above and below the eye
  - centre of circle
  - concentric circles
- Study of the apppearance of rectangular solids at varying angles with the picture plane and at different levels with regard to the eye
- Drawing of the appearance of rectangular solids at an angle of 45° with the picture plane and at different levels with regard to the eye
  - cube
  - square prism
  - square plinth
  - steps
- Groups
  - geometric solids
  - objects based on geometric solids

Drill
- Curves
  - studied from pottery and from examples of Gothic art

The Purposes of this Work are:

To lead the pupils to observe the ever-changing appearances of forms.

To teach them to draw the appearances of rectangular objects at prescribed angles with the picture plane, and to group such objects with others circular in section.

To lead them to see, and to draw such groups as entireties.

To lead them to see the beauty of subtle curvature in objects and in ornaments.

To awaken their desire to reproduce this beauty in their own work.

To train the hands to freedom and precision of movement in drawing these curves.

See remarks on object drawing in eighth year course.

APRIL, MAY, JUNE.

Materials—Clay, paper, pencil, eraser.

Decoration
- Drawings from nature
  - twigs, opposite branching leaves
  - twigs, alternately branching leaves
  - leaves of radical growth
- Conventional bilateral arrangement from natural growth
  - in geometric spaces of various forms and proportions
  - repetitions in borders
- Modeling in clay from nature
  - branch of three or more leaves
- Conventional rosettes
  - from top views of flowers
- Modeling or cutting in clay or other material
  - historic ornament
- Application of design to material
  - outline embroidery
  - applique work on cloth
  - tiles modeled or cut in clay or other material

The Purposes of this Work are:

To lead pupils to observe the laws of growth as illustrated in the branching of trees, and in the radical growth of many plants.

To teach them the application of this law to ornament.

To give them practice in the application of these principles to material that they can handle. (See remarks upon this subject in eight year course.)

EIGHTH YEAR.

SEPTEMBER, OCTOBER, NOVEMBER, DECEMBER.

Time—Three hours per week.
Materials—Model paper, mucilage, two pencils—medium and hard, compasses, practice paper, models, ruler with parts of inches marked and having metal edges.

Free-hand Construction
- Free-hand working-drawings, conventions, section half tinting, etc.
  - hollow cylinder
  - double mortise and tenon T joint

Instrumental Construction
- Geometrical
  - problems 3, 4, 5, 6, 7, 8
- Application of problems 1, 2, 3, 5
  - through dove-tail joint
- Application of problem 7
  - projection of a cube at angles with the picture plane
- Drawing to scale
  - wedge shaped block
  - objects in schoolroom as window, door or side of schoolroom
- Reading working-drawings
  - any suitable working drawings not in this course
- Constructive design
  - pocket-book
  - any object constructed on a similar plan

All that is said in connection with the work in construction in the seventh year work, applies also to the work of this year. Special attention should be given to drawing to scale.

Only such geometric solids as are necessary for models in object drawing need be constructed in this grade. The skeleton forms are useful in this connection. These may be made with cardboard.

The knowledge and skill acquired in making the pocket book may be applied to the making of various articles, as portfolios, book-covers, sachets, envelopes of various patterns, boxes made in one piece, etc. Materials used in patterns of this kind are paper, leather, cloth and tin.

JANUARY, FEBRUARY, MARCH.

Materials—Paper, pencil, eraser, models.

Perspective Representation
- Relative appearance of horizontal faces differing in position and distance
  - two square prisms, vertical and horizontal
  - cylinder and square prism, vertical and horizontal
- Study of objects at varying angles with the picture plane
  - cube
  - plinth
  - books
  - baskets
- Grouping
  - books, vases and other objects similar in character

Drill Exercises
- Curves
  - scroll
  - wave
  - radiating lines

In teaching object drawing the leading purpose should be to develop the ability to see the ever-varying appearances of forms and to lead the pupil through this seeing to recognize the laws that govern the appearances.

The drawing is a description of what is seen and is a necessary step in the process of seeing without which the pupil will not discover his false seeing.

Do not allow the pupil to delude himself with the idea that he sees right, but cannot express it.

If he really sees that a line making a right angle with another appears to make an acute angle, he will not be likely to draw an obtuse or a right angle to represent it, although he may forget if he has only been told that it ought to appear so. After he is sure there is such an appearance he should be taught the reason for it.

Encourage home sketches, and make them occasions for general lessons on the laws governing the appearance of form.

The purpose of the drill exercise is to cultivate freedom and precision of movement in drawing long curves.

The exercise should be carefully studied.

The whole arm movement should be used in the drill.

APRIL, MAY, JUNE.

Materials—Clay, paper, pencil, eraser.

Construction	Modeling from a working-drawing	a paper weight or some similar object
Decoration	Drawing from nature	flowers and leaves showing growth
	Bilateral arrangement	conventional flowers and leaves
	Conventional arrangement showing natural growth	a sprig with a flower and two or three leaves or with flower, buds and leaves
	Combinations	borders; unit and border
	Modeling from nature	flower sprigs; fruits
	Modeling from casts	any good example of historic art, flowers or fruit
	Application of design to material	borders and tiles modeled or carved in clay or other material; designs for embroidery; some article of use as a portfolio or a box designed and constructed from a working drawing in any suitable material and decorated

In drawing plant forms from nature, see that the lesson is given when the sprigs are in good condition.

The sprig to be drawn should be in front of the pupil, and in the water if possible.

The leading lines, the blocking of the general form, and of the leaves and flowers, should be insisted upon before the details are drawn.

Those pupils who cannot work rapidly should be given twigs having fewer leaves or flowers—simpler forms to draw.

It is desirable that each pupil should execute in some material, a design made with the idea of its adaptation to some special purpose. The lesson involved in the exercise is an important one. If clay is selected, architectural ornaments in relief will be especially studied. If embroidery is selected, the attention of the pupil will be directed to the kinds of design suited to different materials and purposes, and correspondingly with any other kinds of work.

As the materials for this work (with the exception of clay) must be provided by the pupils, it cannot be absolutely required. Its introduction must be the result of an interest in the subject aroused by previous lessons, and can only be encouraged and guided by the teacher. It is hoped that the teacher will bear in mind, that encouragement without intelligent direction and criticism, will not accomplish the desired result. If a portfolio or box is chosen, the pupil should be reminded that pleasing proportions in the construction, and a harmonious arrangement of color is of more importance than ornament, and that if an ornament cannot be designed that will add to the beauty of the object, taste in design requires that it should be left without decoration.

Directions for clay modeling will be found in Part II, Appendix B.

Work In Shops.

WOOD.
SEVENTH AND EIGHTH YEARS.

Bench Work:

The correct method of using planes, handsaws, chisels, gouges, brace and bits, hammer, gauge, clamps and other tools, in the working of different kinds of wood.

All construction is from drawings executed by the pupil.

HIGH SCHOOL—FIRST YEAR.

Lathe Work:

The proper use of the hand wood-turning tools in the various operations of turning. Blue-prints used are taken by pupils from their own tracings and drawings.

SECOND YEAR.

IRON.

Forging:

The making and management of a forge fire and the forging of small articles of iron involving all fundamental operations.

Steel tool-making, hardening and temporing.

THIRD AND FOURTH YEARS.

Machine-tool Work:

The use of engine-lathe, planer, sharper, drill-press and hand-lathe, in the various processes of metal turning, boring, thread-cutting, planing, slotting, drilling, polishing, etc., upon cast-iron, wrought-iron, steel, brass and composition.

See Teacher's Manual, pamphlet form.

Cooking.

SEVENTH AND EIGHTH YEARS.

The object of the course is to give the pupils instruction in plain cooking and in housekeeping, so far as it is dependent on the kitchen. In addition to recipes for ordinary dishes, and making and cooking the same in the school, notes are given on the proper way of mixing ingredients, and on the best manner of arranging and preserving provisions. As much of the chemistry of food is taught as is necessary for intelligent cooking.

Two hours a week throughout the two years.

See Teacher's Manual, pamphlet form.

Sewing.

THIRD YEAR.

Basting.
Running.
Stitching.
Overcasting.
Hemming—three widths, ⅛, ½ and 1 inch.
Top sewing.
Work bag.

FOURTH YEAR.

Teach bias *fell*.
French seam.
Tucking.
Gathering—plain and French.
Patching.
Button-holes.
Drafting of seamless waist and making of same.

FIFTH YEAR.

Gussets.
Button-holes and buttons.
Cloth darning—with and without piece; straight and three-cornered.
Garment mending—both patching and darning.
Hem-stitching.
Feather-stitching.
Herring-bone stitch.
Draft skirt and make same.

SIXTH YEAR.

Button-holes—cotton and cloth.
Stocking darning.
Draft drawers and make same.
Drafting of sleeve.
Cutting and fitting by measurement, from "The M. O. Jones Self-adjusting Tailor System," as taught in the sixth grades, in the southeast and southwest sections of the city.

Music.

The immediate purpose of the work in music is to develop pure, full voices, to train the pupils to read music accurately at sight, and to sing with intelligence and feeling.

A full explanation of the methods to be pursed in this work is to be found in the Music Manual.

MATERIAL.

In each school-room there should be a pitch pipe and a simple pendulum, permanently suspended from the wall. On the blackboard, in all schools, throughout the year, there should be a representation on the staff, of the major scale, in the various keys. (Modulator.) In all schools above the third grade, a similar representation of the chromatic scale should also be kept on the board.

Exercise cards, showing the methodical development of interval work in the major, minor and chromatic scales are furnished for the guidance of teachers. Exercise cards are also furnished to aid in the introduction and development of two-part and three-part harmony.

The schools are supplied with sight work arranged for the introduction and thorough development of the representation of each new step in the study of intervals and time. For the first and second grades, printed sheets of music, from which, each day, exercises are to be copied on the board, are furnished for the teachers. For the other grades, the sight work is printed for each child. Above the second grade this work is supplemented by parallel work in the singing books. Each group of sight work is accompanied by a card designating what music in the books should be sung in connection with it.

Songs for rote work are supplied for the first six grades.

All the sight work supplied should be sung. The rote songs should be taught as directed by the special teacher.

SCHEDULE OF WORK.

FIRST YEAR.

First Term:

The scale should be taught as a unit. The intervals of the lower part of the scale (1-5, inclusive) should then be studied.

The idea of two-part time should be developed,

Second Term:

The study of the lower part of the scale should be continued. The intervals in the upper part of the scale (five to eight inclusive) should be studied at first separately, and then in connection with those of the lower.

The sight work consists of exercises involving (1) only those intervals with which the children should be familiar and (2) the one form in time (quarter notes in 2-4 time) which they know perfectly.

The idea of quarter rests should be developed toward the end of this term.

Third Term:

The more difficult intervals of the scale should be studied. At the end of the term the pupils should be able to sing any interval of the major scale.

The sight work introduces the new intervals learned and the new time character—the quarter rest.

Rote songs throughout the year.

SECOND YEAR.

First Term:

The first year's work should be reviewed until the children can take any interval of the major scale and can sing, at sight, exercises in 2-4 time containing only quarter notes and quarter rests.

Tones above and below the keynote should be studied in their relations to each other.

The idea of half notes and half rests in 2-4 time should be developed.

Second Term:

The study of intervals should be kept up with great care. The vowels should be used more than the syllables in this work.

The sight-work consists of exercises using the time form already familiar, together with the newly developed time characters—the half note and the half rest. The tie is introduced here.

Third Term:

The previous work with intervals should be continued. The names of the intervals—major second, minor second, etc.—should be taught.

The sight-work consists of more difficult exercises, involving the use of the time form and the time characters—already familiar. The use of the hold is taught.

Rote songs throughout the year.

THIRD YEAR.

First Term:

The work of the previous years should be reviewed until the children can sing any exercise written in 2-4 time, using only quarter notes, quarter rests, half notes and half rests, with the tie and hold.

The intervals of the minor scale should be studied.

The idea of four-part time should be developed.

Second Term:

The study of intervals in the major and minor scales should be continued with unceasing care. Knowing the intervals by name, the children should be taught to sing any interval from a given note as the name of the interval is called. Two-part harmony should be added to the interval work.

The sight work is in 4-4 time, using quarter notes, quarter rests, half notes, half rests, and developing the new characters—the dotted half note, the whole note and whole rest.

The idea of three-part time should be developed.

Third Term:

The previous interval work should be continued. Two-part harmony should be developed further. In addition, the children should be taught to recognize and name the various intervals when heard.

The sight work is in 3-4 time, involving the characters already familiar. In this term also occur easy exercises in two-part harmony, in two, three and four part time.

Rote songs throughout the year.

FOURTH YEAR.

First Term:

The work of the previous years should be reviewed until the children can read readily exercises in 2-4, 4-4 and 3-4 time, using quarter, half and whole notes, the corresponding rests and the dotted half note.

The easier intervals of the chromatic scale should be studied.

The sight work is written chiefly in 3-8 time, developing the idea of the eighth note, eighth rest and the dotted quarter note. The greater part of the sight work from now on is written for two parts.

Second Term:

The interval work should be continued along the same lines as in first term work. The study of the chromatic scale should be further developed.

The sight work develops 6-8 time.

Third Term:

The intervals of the major, minor and chromatic scales should still be diligently studied.

The sight work develops the eighth note and eighth rest in 2-4, 3-4 and 4-4 time.

Rote songs throughout the year.

FIFTH YEAR.

First Term:

The work should be reviewed until the children can sing sight exercises in 2-4, 4-4, 3-4, 3-8 and 6-8 time, using whole, half, quarter and eighth notes, their corresponding rests, and the dotted half note; also the dotted quarter note in 3-8 and 6-8 time.

Second Term:

Advanced interval work in the major, minor and chromatic scales.

The sight work develops the dotted quarter note in 2-4, 3-4 and 4-4 time.

Third Term:

Advanced interval work.

The sight work develops the sixteenth note in 2-4, 4-4, 3-4, 3-8 and 6-8 time.

Rote songs throughout the year.

SIXTH YEAR.

First Term:

The work of the previous year should be thoroughly reviewed.

Three-part harmony should be introduced in the interval work.

Second Term:

Advanced interval work in the major, minor and chromatic scales. Three-part harmony should be developed further.

The sight work develops the dotted eighth in the various kinds of time already presented. The sight work is now written chiefly for three parts.

Third Term:

- Advanced interval work.

The sight work develops the thirty-second note and the dotted sixteenth note in the different kinds of time already presented.

Rote songs throughout the year.

SEVENTH YEAR.

The work of the sixth grade should be thoroughly reviewed.

The study of intervals in the major, minor and chromatic scales should be continued faithfully.

A sufficient number of exercises should be given in 2-2, 2-8, 6-4, 9-8 and 12-8 time to render the pupils sufficiently familiar with those time-forms to sing them understandingly and with ease.

The simple marks of expression, as pp, p, f, ff, etc., are taught incidentally in the work of the previous years. In this grade the signs indicating the degrees of force, as crescendo, decrescendo, swell, pressure, tone, forzando, staccato, marcato, legato, etc., as well as terms indicating the character of the movement, such as andante, adagio, allegro, etc., should be introduced.

EIGHTH YEAR.

The work of the seventh grade should be reviewed. The work with intervals should be continued.

The double sharp, double flat and double natural should be introduced.

The study of thirds in the different kinds of time should be taken up.

The more difficult forms of syncopation should be studied.

In addition to this work a large amount of music should be sung, especial attention being given to expression.

Health Exercises.

I. INTRODUCTION.

II. AIMS.

III. GENERAL GROUPING OF EXERCISES.
    1 Stretching Exercises
    2 Exercises for Strength
    3 Relaxing Exercises
    4 Exercises for Grace
    5 Breathing Exercises
    6 Vocal Exercises.

IV. GENERAL DIRECTIONS.

V. POSITIONS AND SIGNALS.

VI. FIRST AND SECOND GRADES.

VII. THIRD AND FOURTH GRADES.

VIII. FIFTH AND SIXTH GRADES.

IX. SEVENTH AND EIGHTH GRADES.

I. INTRODUCTION.

A manual of physical culture which will present the work in its entirety, is now in course of preparation. This will contain a graded course with full and definite instructions for giving the same.

As heretofore, the teachers will continue to work from printed lesson sheets containing daily programs of lessons given by the teachers of physical culture.

II. AIMS.

1. General:

The general aim of physical culture is to secure that perfect condition of the body that is conducive to its best use in everyday life.

2. Specific:

    1 Health
    2 Good carriage of body
    3 Symetrical development
    4 Grace
    5 A good speaking voice

III. GENERAL GROUPING OF EXERCISES.

According to the purpose of the exercises, and the principles upon which they are based, the following general grouping can be made.

1. Stretching Exercises:

These counteract the effect of the overuse of the flexor rather than of the extensor muscles.

2. Exercises for Strength:

These are given to make the muscles obedient to the will, and to secure organic perfection of the body.

They are given in the order of the parts of the body, thereby tending to secure an even development.

3. Relaxing Exercises:

By these the body is relieved of unnecessary tension and prepared for graceful movements.

4. **Exercises for Grace:**

Graceful movements are seen and imitated by the children.

5. **Breathing Exercises:**
   a For the thorough expansion of the lungs.
   b To give control of the breath, making a basis for vocal work.

6. **Vocal Exercises:**

Exercises adapted to the grade are given in breathing, in articulating, in tone-placing and in pronouncing. A good speaking voice is all that is sought.

According to the parts of the body exercised, groups 1, 2, and 3 are in the main capable of the following division:

1 Head

2 Trunk
- Chest
- Back
- Waist
- Abdomen

3 Upper Limbs
- Arm
- Forearm
- Hand

4 Lower Limbs
- Thigh
- Leg
- Foot

GENERAL DIRECTIONS.

I. The average amount of time to be devoted to gymnastic work in each grade is from 15 to 20 minutes daily.

```
1st grade---------------19 minutes.
2d    "  ---------------19    "
3d    "  ---------------25    "
4th   "  ---------------24    "
5th   "  ---------------14    "
6th   "  ---------------14    "
7th   "  ---------------12    "
8th   "  ---------------18    "
```

II. The best results can be obtained by giving the exercises at 10 o'clock in the morning, or midway between the forenoon recess and the noon hour, or at 2 o'clock in the afternoon.

Decide upon a certain time in the daily program when the exercises are to be given, then give them at that time with the regularity of the daily recess.

III. If, at the beginning of school in the morning, the upper sashes of the windows are lowered a short and equal distance, such as can be maintained during the day, a constant ventilation of the school-room will be secured. This refers to buildings that are not automatically ventilated.

Before beginning the gymnastic work each time let monitors, appointed for that purpose, lower the windows a greater distance.

When exercising, the temperature of the room should be between 65° and 70°.

IV. Use every reasonable influence to persuade the girls to adopt a loose style of dress for the school-room.

V. The appearance of the class is improved and better gymnastic work secured, if the pupils are seated according to height with the shortest in front.

VI. Study the lesson sheet carefully before attempting to give a new lesson.

Know the name of each exercise and the correct signals for the same.

See that the children know the names of the exercises, the signals, and what to do when the signals are given.

VII. Avoid all unnecessary movements during gymnastic exercises. All muscles not being used should be at rest.

VIII. If, for any reason, a change in the lesson is desirable, see that an exercise be given for each part of the body.

IX. Induce the pupils to maintain a good carriage of the body at all times.

When passing in line, each pupil should keep the distance of the length of the arm or of the forearm from the one in front of him.

Cultivate the habit of walking in a straight line.

X. Teach the pupils, when walking up and down stairs, to hold the body erect, placing the ball of the foot first on the step.

XI. A practical application of the lesson in rising, sitting, standing, walking, ascending and descending steps, should be insisted upon at all times during the day, thereby forming correct habits.

XII. When criticizing a lesson as a whole, the following points are specially noted :

1. Ventilation
2. Positions { eyes, head, chest, hands, feet }
   a Sitting
   b Standing
3. Accuracy
   a Of the class as a whole
   b Of individual pupils
4. Method of teacher
5. Uniformity
6. Quietness

POSITIONS AND SIGNALS.

Sitting Position:

I. Resting Position
  1 Body far back in the seat with back resting
  2 Chest raised
  3 Head erect
  4 Eyes looking toward the front
  5 Hands resting in the lap
  6 Feet on the floor, one slightly in advance of the other

II. Upright Position :
  1 Body in an erect position, far back in the seat
  2 In other respects the "Upright Position" is similar to the "Resting Position."

The "Upright Position" is always to be taken during gymnastic work in the seats, and when preparing to rise.

Practice changing from "Resting Position" to "Upright Position."

Use the Signals "Rest" and "Upright" to designate these two positions.

Standing Positions:

I. Position of respect.
   1 Chest raised
   2 Abdomen held well back
   3 Weight resting mainly on the balls of the feet
   4 Head erect
   5 Arms relaxed at sides
   6 Feet forming an angle of about 60°
   7 Eyes looking toward the front.

II. Speaker's position.
   1 One foot in advance, so that the heel of the forward foot is opposite the instep of the other foot
   2 Most of the weight on the ball of the forward foot

In other respects the "Speaker's Position" is similar to the "Position of Respect."

SIGNALS.

When the class rises in a body the signals to be given are as follows:

I. Rising.

1. "Ready"—Place the right foot in the aisle.
2. "Rise"—Rise, bringing the left foot up to the right foot and take "Position of Respect."
3. "Position"—Step into the middle of the aisle, taking "Position of Respect" directly behind the pupil in front.

II. Sitting.

1. "Ready"—Take a step beside the seat, bringing heels together.
2. "Sit"—Place the left foot in front of the seat and sit.
3. "Position"—Take "Resting Position."

Practice rising toward the left.

FIRST AND SECOND YEARS.

The exercises given to the children in the first and second years of school work have largely the elements of play, involving however, the necessary preparation for the regular gymnastic work beginning in the third grade.

These may be considered as :

I. Hygienic—seeking a good carriage and a regular development with all possible conditions of the school-room secured, which aid in the child's healthful growth.

II. Recreative—seeking to obtain in play that exercise which is most natural.

Gymnastic Games:

Games which exercise many parts of the body, and in which all of the pupils can take part, are to be introduced during the year.

Positions:

Begin at once to teach correct positions for sitting and standing.

First show what you wish by setting the example, then let the children imitate.

Select the best examples from the class to be observed and imitated by the pupils.

Finally, give individual attention wherever it is necessary.

When ready for work the children should have the best standing position in the middle of the aisle. The line should be straight and graded according to height.

Signals:

Teach the signals for rising and sitting. Try to obtain uniformity by having each pupil move with the one in front.

Stretching Exercises:

Much stretching of all parts of the body is good. It is profitable to have these exercises after lessons in penmanship and drawing.

Relaxing Exercises:

Frequently lift the arms of pupils when standing and walking, to see if they drop lifelessly.

Be careful that pupils do not raise the shoulders thinking that thereby they are raising the chest. To correct this evil give relaxing exercises for the shoulders.

Walking:

First let one row walk around the room. The children who are sitting in their seats should observe and decide who walk the best.

When two rows are able to walk well, unite them and form one line.

Finally let the whole school walk around the room.

The children should know and observe the following directions:

1. Keep the chest high
2. Hold the head erect
3. Carry the arms loosely at the sides
4. Walk in a straight line
5. Turn a square corner
6. Keep the distance of the length of the arm or of the forearm from the child in front.

Exercises for Grace:

Natural movements and attitudes which do not violate the principles of grace are given by the teacher to be imitated by the children.

Breathing:

A few natural deep breaths taken in an upright position at the direction of the teacher, is all that is expected in these grades.

Voice:

Secure soft, clear and smooth tones in the school-room by giving them for the imitation of the children.

THIRD AND FOURTH YEARS.

The gymnastics now take on the character of accuracy and precision.

Positions:

The positions to be taken for gymnastics, both when sitting and standing, have been taught in the first and second grades and now need to be insisted upon that correct habits may be formed.

Signals:

These are to be given as drill exercises until the whole class is able to move with ease, uniformity, and quietness. Do not permit the children when rising to help themselves by taking hold of the desk. The arms should drop at the sides, and the best standing position immediately be taken beside the seat, without fussing or unnecessary movements of the body.

Exercise for Strength:

These exercises, with full directions, will be printed on the lesson sheets issued during the year.

Relaxing Exercises:

Relax hands before and after lessons in penmanship and drawing.

Elevated shoulders can be brought down and a stiff carriage of the arms overcome by giving relaxing exercises for these parts.

Walking:

Frequently let the children walk for the observation and criticism of the whole class. Each child should know and observe the following points:
1 Head erect
2 Chest high
3 Abdomen held well back
4 Arms hanging loosely
5 Walk lightly.

Breathing:

Give breathing exercises each day taken in an upright position.

Breathe deep, so as to thoroughly expand the lungs.

Voice:

To secure a good natural tone, the child should be in a good humor, without frowns or unpleasant feelings.

Cultivate the ear of each pupil by presenting good, clear, smooth tones for imitation.

FIFTH AND SIXTH YEARS.

As the work advances a few of the simple exercises are combined requiring greater co-operation of muscles. Lead the children to see the relation of physical exercises to good health.

Teach the importance of a good carriage as affecting health and as a matter of personal appearance.

Positions and Signals:

The remarks made in regard to positions and signals in the work for the first four grades apply to these grades.

Exercises for Strength:

Always give these in the order of the parts of the body, so that at the end of the lesson the whole of the body will have been exercised.

Walking:

Observe all the directions given in regard to a good carriage. Cultivate the habit of walking directly forward in a straight line.

When children walk in a line, for the sake of appearance, the following directions should be obeyed:

1. Keep the distance of the length of the arm or of the forearm from the one in front.
2. Walk directly behind the one in front, so as to keep the line straight.
3. Turn square corners.

Ascending and Descending Steps:

It is well, as an exercise, to let the whole school pass out of the room, down and up stairs, observing the points given above. When going upstairs bear in mind to keep the body erect and place the ball of the foot first on the step.

Relaxing Exercises:

Frequently practice the relaxing exercises given during the year, even after perfection is obtained.

Breathing:

Let the children place their hands on the waist in front so as to feel the motion at that part.

During breathing there should be little or no motion of the shoulders.

Voice:

Breathing exercises, in which the breath is exhaled very slowly, are given to gain control of the muscles used in exhalation, thereby gaining control of the breath.

Simple exercises in articulation are given during the year.

It is suggested that lists of mispronounced words be kept on the board, and that frequently the pupils be drilled in pronouncing them correctly and distinctly.

SEVENTH AND EIGHTH YEARS.

The work in these grades presents greater difficulties, including many combined exercises.

It is desirable that the children have a distinct understanding of all that is done.

Teach in connection with physiology :

1 The relation of exercises to health
2 The value of special exercises, or school gymnastics, given for the symmetrical development of the body

3 The importance of a good carriage of the body—
  a For health
  b For personal appearance
4 The hygienic value of deep breathing
5 The injurious effects of tight clothing

In the eighth grade the pupils ought to understand the physiology of breathing—the muscles used in respiration, and their action in inhalation and exhalation.

Positions:

The children know the essentials of a good standing position. This should be insisted on at all times until the habit is fixed.

Take many exercises with a book on the head. This will most quickly and surely secure a good general carriage.

Signals:

When perfection has been obtained in obeying signals, not more than a minute need be spent in passing from the best sitting position to the best standing position.

When rising, avoid bending forward more than is necessary. Avoid also the other extreme, rising without any motion of the spinal column.

Exercises for Strength:

One day each week is to be spent in exercises with wands or dumb-bells.

Other exercises of the week will be printed on daily programs.

Walking:

Teach pupils as individuals to walk lightly, freely swinging the leg from the hip, and without unnecessary motion in the upper part of the body. However, in walking, as in all exercises, avoid a stiff carriage of the spine and head.

Ascending and Descending Steps:

Frequently let the whole class pass out of the room, down and up stairs, observing the directions given to the fifth and sixth grades for these drills.

Relaxing Exercises:

Whenever a stiffness of any part of the body, caused by unnecessary tension, is noticed, immediately give a relaxing exercise for that part of the body.

Voice:

The voice work in these grades may be considered under four heads :
1 Breathing.
    a For the thorough expansion of the lungs.
    b To strengthen the muscles of respiration and give control of the breath during exhalation.
2 Tone placing.
    To secure a good tone, the breath should be directed well forward in the mouth. Exercises are given to cultivate the tendency to throw the tone there.
3 Articulation.
    Exercises are given to cultivate a prompt but easy action of the organs of articulations, avoiding too great precision of utterance.
4 Pronunciation.
    At the beginning of the week place on the board a list of words commonly mispronounced. Drill the pupils in uttering them correctly and distinctly one minute each day.

HIGH SCHOOLS.

The Studies of the Academic High Schools embrace Mathematics, Physics, Chemistry, Mineralogy, Natural History (Botany, Zoölogy), Geology, History, Political Science, English, German, Latin, Drawing, Manual Training, Military Drill and Vocal Music. For convenience of classification, two leading courses of study are outlined, but no one of these is in every part compulsory. Subject to the requirements of the hour plan of recitations, a pupil, acting with the approval of his parents or guardian, may determine his own course of study. The order of subjects in the several departments, with the hours of recitation or number of exercises apportioned to each, is as follows:

MATHEMATICS.

FIRST YEAR.

School Algebra, Wentworth—Simultaneous simple equations; Involution and evolution; Radical expressions; Quadratic equations; Theory of exponents; Ratio and Proportion; Progressions; Binomial Theorem. *One hundred and eighty hours.*

SECOND YEAR.

Plane Geometry, Wentworth—Rectilinear figures; Circles; Proportional lines and similar polygons; Comparison and measurement of the surfaces of polygons; Regular polygons and circles.
Theorems for original demonstration.
Exercises involving the practical application of propositions proved. *One hundred and twenty-four hours.*
Solid Geometry, Wentworth—Lines and Planes in Space. *Twenty hours.*

THIRD YEAR.

Solid Geometry, Wentworth — Polyhedral angles; Polyhedrons, cylinders and cones; The sphere.
Original demonstrations and exercises as in the second year. *Forty-four hours.*
Plane Trigonometry—Functions of acute angles; The right triangle; Goniometry; The oblique triangle. *Forty-four hours.*
Surveying, with Field-work—Instruments and their uses; Land surveying; Triangulation; Leveling; Railroad surveying.

Field-work with the compass, transit, plane-table and level.
Computation and plotting from field notes. *Fifty-six hours.*

FOURTH YEAR.

Analytical Geometry, Wentworth—Plotting of curves; Relation of pole and polars of a circle; Parabola; Locus of middle points of parallel chords; Tangents from ends of chords, ellipse, hyperbole, asymptotes, conjugate diameters, etc. *Eighty-eight hours.*

College Algebra, Wentworth—*Fifty-six hours.*

CHEMISTRY.

SECOND YEAR.

Inorganic Chemistry, Eliot and Storer's Manual. *Thirty-six hours.*
Introduction to Organic Chemistry.
Experimental Lectures, reported by students. *Thirty-six hours.*
Laboratory Practice. *One hundred and five hours.*

THIRD YEAR.

Organic Chemistry, Eliot and Storer's Manual.
Laboratory Practice in Analytical Chemistry. *One hundred and five hours.*
Qualitative Analysis.
Experimental Lectures, reported by students. *Thirty-six hours.*

FOURTH YEAR.

Organic Chemistry.
Assaying.
Quantitative Analysis.

MINERALOGY.

THIRD YEAR.

Crosby's Mineralogy. *Fifteen hours.*
Blowpipe Analysis and Determinative Mineralogy. *Sixty hours.*
Study of collection at the National Museum.
Preparations of specimens for the school cabinet.

PHYSICS.*

SECOND YEAR.

Gage's Introduction to Physical Science. *Seventy-two hours.*
Lectures, with Experiments. *Twenty hours.*
Laboratory. *One hundred and five hours.*

---

*NOTE.—A continuous effort is made, throughout the course, to develop habits of personal investigation, and each student is encouraged to make and to use the most instructive pieces of physical apparatus. The appliances at hand in the Department of Manual Training are utilized to this end, thus combining the practice of the training of both branches.

THIRD YEAR.

Gage's Introduction to Physical Science, (continued).
Lodge's Elements of Mechanics, Light, Heat, Sound, Thompson's Elementary Lessons in Electricity.
Recitations. *Thirty-five hours.*
Laboratory. *One hundred and forty hours.*

FOURTH YEAR.

Laboratory.
Electricity and Magnetism. *One hundred and forty-four hours.*

ZOÖLOGY.*

FIRST YEAR.

Zoölogy—Work in Examinations of Objects, with and without the microscope. *Twenty hours.*
Packard's First Lesson in Zoölogy. *Twenty hours.*
Laboratory Practice. *Thirty-six hours.*
Studies at the U. S. Fish Commission Station, the Smithsonian Institution and National Museum. *Ten hours.*
Preparation of a Paper Stating Results of Original Observations on a special topic assigned.
Preparations of a Condensed Summary of the Characters of Principal Orders throughout the Animal Kingdom.

BOTANY.*

THIRD YEAR.

Botany—Practical Exercises in the Examination and Analysis of Plants. *Eighty hours.*
Gray's Lessons and Manual. *Forty hours.*
Lectures (supplementary to the text-books, and upon Cryptogams). *Forty hours.*
Laboratory Work (devoted to exercises in drawing and describing the details of plant structure, with and without the microscope). *Thirty hours.*
Study of Tropical Plants and of Growing Plants.
Studies at the U. S. Botanical Gardens and in Excursions.
Preparation of 100 Description Papers (each stating the characteristic external features of some plant analyzed).
Preparation of 3 Observation Papers (stating results of original observation on some general topic assigned).
Preparation of a Condensed Summary of Structural and Systematic Botany.

---

*NOTE.—In these subjects, as will be seen from above, the mode of study is founded on the examination of subjects, with the constant aim of developing the habit of observation.

Preparation of Illustrative charts, in crayon, colored chalk and water color.

FOURTH YEAR.

Advanced Botany—Trees and Plants of Washington. *Sixty hours.*
Laboratory Work, with and without the microscope, using Bower's Practical Botany. *Sixty hours.*

GEOLOGY.*

FOURTH YEAR.

Geology—Le Conte's Elements. *Sixty hours.*
Laboratory Work—*Sixty hours.*

HISTORY AND POLITICAL SCIENCE.†

FIRST YEAR.

Oriental History.
History of Greece.
    Myers' The Eastern Nations and Greece. Four hours weekly, first half year. *Seventy-two hours.*
History of Rome.
    Allen's Short History of the Roman People. Four hours weekly, second half year. *Seventy-two hours.*

SECOND YEAR.

Montgomery's History of England. Three hours weekly. *One hundred and eight hours.*

THIRD YEAR.

Myers' General History.
Fiske's Civil Government in the United States. Four hours weekly. *One hundred and forty-four hours.*

FOURTH YEAR.

American History and Constitution: by topics. Four hours weekly. *One hundred and forty-four hours.*
Political Economy. Four hours weekly. *One hundred and forty-four hours.*

---

*NOTE.—In this subject, as will be seen from above, the mode of study is founded on the examination of subjects, with the constant aim of developing the habit of observation.

†NOTE.—The general method of instruction lays stress upon the value of topical studies. These vary in character in the different years, but all have the aim to teach the students the art of using advantageously sources of information, the power of discriminating between important and unimportant facts, and the habit of clear and forcible expression of ideas.

ENGLISH.

FIRST YEAR.

Representative Discourse. Structure and Expression—description, narration, comparison and exposition. *Twenty-seven hours.*
Brief outline of English Literature. *Twelve hours.*
Selections from Standard Authors. *Seventy hours.*
Tennyson.
Dickens.
Macaulay.
Coleridge.
Byron.
Goldsmith, etc.

SECOND YEAR.

Argumentative Discourse—proofs, *a priori*, proofs by example, proofs by evidence. *Eighteen hours.*
Principles of Rhetoric. *Thirty-six hours.*
Addison. Milton. *Eighteen hours.*
Shakespeare—(comedy). *Thirty-six hours.*

THIRD YEAR.

Chaucer. Prologue and Nonnes Tale. *Twenty-eight hours.*
Bacon. Essays. *Twenty-four hours.*
Milton. Paradise Lost. *Twenty hours.*
Shakespeare (tragedy). *Seventy-two hours.*

FOURTH YEAR.

The English Essayists. *Thirty-six hours.*
The English Novel. *Thirty-six hours.*
Topics for Research, Criticism and Invention, connected with a study of Modern Poetry and a review of Grammar and Rhetoric. *Seventy-two hours.*

NOTE.—The first year's course aims to instruct pupils in the art of writing and speaking correct English, to give a knowledge of what is best in literature, and to cultivate a love for books and reading. An entire selection is taken for critical study. The principles of correct expression are impressed by constant exercises in writing. Pupils are required to keep note-books, in which outlines, reproductions, notes of lectures, and tables are entered.

In the second year the study of Rhetoric is supplemented by reference to the best English writers, for practical examples, and by constant practice in writing.

Shakespeare is studied with a view to broad literary culture. An entire quarter is devoted to a single play, which is so presented as to evolve an appreciation of the art of dramatic composition and the development of character and plot, as also original critical thought in pupils.

The course in English is progressive, the first year's work being preparatory to the second, the second to the third, etc.

GERMAN.

FIRST YEAR.

Bernhardt's "Sprach und Lesebuch," Vol I; Conversation; Writing German; Stories. *One hundred and eighty hours.*
Storm's "Immensee."

SECOND YEAR.

Bernhardt's "Sprachbuch," Vol. II; "Im Zwielicht," Vol. I; Geschichte der deutschen Litteratur; Conversation; Composition; Grammar. *One hundred and forty-four hours.*

THIRD YEAR.

Bernhardt's "Goethe's Meisterwerke;" Geschichte der deutschen Litteratur; Conversation; Advanced Composition; Grammar. *One hundred and forty-four hours.*

FOURTH YEAR.

Sheldon's German Grammar.
Goethe's Meisterwerke—complete.
Selections from Schiller.
Lessing's "Nathan der Weise."

LATIN.

FIRST YEAR.

Grammar and Lessons. *One hundred and forty hours.*
Gallic War, Book II, ten chapters. *Forty hours.*

SECOND YEAR.

Gallic War, Books I, II, III and IV. *One hundred and forty hours.*
Cicero, One Oration. *Forty-five hours.*

THIRD YEAR.

Cicero, Seven Orations. *One hundred and twenty hours.*
Æneid, Book I. *Sixty hours.*

FOURTH YEAR.

Æneid, Books II, III, IV, V and VI. Eclogues.
Ovid, Reviews.
Collar's Composition. *One hour per week,* first semester of last three years.
Writing Latin and reading at sight, throughout the course, and occasional lectures on Latin literature, antiquities, and philology.

GREEK.

SECOND YEAR.

White's First Lessons. *Seventy-two hours.*
Xenophon's Anabasis.—Book I, begun.

THIRD YEAR.

Xenophon's Anabasis.—Books I, II, III, IV, and review.
Goodwin's Grammar.

FOURTH YEAR.

Goodwin's Greek Moods and Tenses.
Herodotus—Book VII.
Homer's Iliad.—Books I, II, III, IV.
Prose Composition.

DRAWING.

Regular Classes.

FIRST YEAR.

One hour per week.

Geometrical work.—Construction of geometrical problems; geometrical design; development of solids; making models of paper to be used in free-hand work.

Free-hand work.—Review and study of cube, square prism, cylinder, cone, triangular prism, hexagonal prism, and square, pyramid, groups of models in different positions and shaded in one tone; sketching flowers and leaves from nature.

SECOND YEAR:

One hour per week.

Geometrical work.—Study of Roman letters; orthographic projection; development of solids and making models of paper.

Free-hand work.—Study of groups of models and school-room objects, with light and shade effects; flower drawing from nature.

THIRD YEAR:

One hour per week.

Geometrical work.—Review of projections; study of mechanical perspective, both parallel and angular; the rule for finding the real length of a line from its projections and its application in the development of pyramidal forms.

Free-hand work.—Groups of models and other objects drawn on paper with charcoal, or on the blackboard, to acquire breadth of treatment.

FOURTH YEAR.

One hour per week.

Sketching from inanimate objects and from life, using soft pencil or charcoal.

Elective Course.

FIRST YEAR.

Two hours per week.
- *Geometrical work.*—Study of polygons, ellipse, parabola, hyperbola, cycloid curves, Roman and Greek moldings, etc.
- *Free-hand work.*—Study in light and shade, single models, groups of models, and Greek vase forms, using pencil and pen and ink; study of plant drawing from nature.
- *Clay work*—Modeling Greek vase forms in the round; modeling in relief forms from casts and from the natural leaf.

SECOND YEAR:

Two hours per week.
- *Geometrical work.*—Projections, orthographic and isometric; perspective, by direct use of projections and by use of vanishing points and measuring points.
- *Free-hand work.*—Study of light and shade, shading with stump, single objects, groups of objects, Greek vase forms and simple casts.
- *Clay work.*—Modeling in the round the Greek vase forms studied in light and shade; designing a simple rosette form and modeling it in relief.

THIRD YEAR:

Two hours per week. Three elective courses.
- *Geometrical work.*—Continue work of previous year in projections, with light and shade, using water-color washes.
- Study helix and screws (wooden and iron).
- Study development of solids, making paper model—cones showing parabola, hyperbola, ellipse; roofs with dormer windows; one prism penetrated by another, etc.
- *Crayon work.*—Continue work of second year, using more elaborate casts of fruit and flowers, of the parts of the human face; masks of classic heads, and busts.
- Clay work: Modeling from casts the parts of the human face and masks in connection with the study of light and shade from the same casts.
- *Water-color work.*—Painting groups of objects first in monochrome, then in color; flowers from nature; study of historical ornament and original design, modeling, design in relief.

FOURTH YEAR.

Time, two hours per week.
Advanced work, in color, crayon, or geometrical drawing.

VOCAL MUSIC.

FIRST YEAR.

Drill in the elementary principles of music; Sight reading; Part songs. *One hour a week.*

SECOND AND THIRD YEARS.

Sight reading, continued; Part songs; Chorals; Glees. *One hour a week.*

FOURTH YEAR.

Drill in expression and the finer points of execution.

MANUAL TRAINING.

FIRST YEAR.

Drawing. *Twenty hours.*
Wood-turning. *Sixty hours.*

SECOND YEAR.

Blacksmithing. *Sixty hours.*
Drawing. *Twenty hours.*

THIRD YEAR.

Machine shop work. *Eighty to two hundred hours.*

FOURTH YEAR.

Continuation of work in the Machine Shop. *Eighty to two hundred hours.*

MILITARY DRILL.

The organization for this purpose consists of a regiment of two battalions, of four companies each, with a full roster of field, staff, and line officers, and membership is open to all boys of suitable age and size, not physically disqualified.

Drills occur twice a week, beginning at two o'clock.

The public exhibitions and parades in which the battalion may participate are limited to the following:

(a) An exhibition drill at some convenient time near the close of the school year, at which the various companies compete for a prize flag for excellence in drill.

(b) A dress parade near the close of the year, when the battalion is reviewed by the District Commissioners and the Secretary of War.

The school makes arrangements to have uniforms furnished at contract price, usually not exceeding $15.00.

The equipment of the battalion consists of Springfield cadet rifles and regulation accoutrements.

THE SCHOOL LIBRARY.

Use of the school library is prescribed in connection with the courses of study.

Books are arranged and catalogued by subjects.

Cyclopedias and works of reference are for consultation only; other books may be drawn.

Number of volumes in library, five thousand six hundred.

Hours for pupils, from two to half-past three o'clock each school-day.

Pupils have access to the library during their study periods in school hours by securing permit slips from teacher.

The librarian and an assistant teacher are always present to direct and assist pupils.

TEXT-BOOKS AUTHORIZED FOR USE.

IN THE FIRST-YEAR CLASS.

English: Pamphlets in English Classic Series (may be procured as needed). *Smith's English and American Literature, 80 cts. *History:* Myer's Eastern Nations and Greece, $1.00. Allen's History of the Roman People, $1.00. *Algebra:* Wentworth's School, $1.15. *Latin:* Allen & Greenough's Grammar (Revised,) $1.25. The Beginners' Latin Book, Collar and Daniell, $1.00. *German:* Bernhardt's Sprachbuch, I, $1.10; "Immensee," 30 and 50 cts. *Zoölogy:* Packard's Elementary Course, 90 cts. *Drawing:* Blank Drawing Book (manilla paper).

BUSINESS COURSE.—*Business Arithmetic:* Sadler's Inductive, Part II, 90 cts. *English:* Eaton's Manual of Correspondence, 25 cts. Lockwood's Lessons in English, $1.25. *Book-keeping:* Bryant and Stratton's Common School, 85 cts. *Shorthand:* Barnes' Manual, 90 cts.

IN THE SECOND-YEAR CLASS.

English: A. S. Hill's Principles of Rhetoric, 80 cts. *History:* Montgomery's English History, $1.12. *Chemistry:* Eliot and Storer's Manual (last edition) $1.15. *Geometry:* Wentworth's New Plane and Solid, (Revised) $1.40. *Latin:* Cæsar's Gallic War (any edition, Kelsey's or Allen & Greenough's recommended), $1.25. *Greek:* Goodwin's Greek Grammar (edition of '92), $1.50. White's Greek Lessons, $1.20. *German:* Bernhardt's Sprachbuch, II, $1.10. "Im Zwielicht" Vol. I, 75 cts. Die Geschichte der deutschen Litteratur. *Heath's German-English and English-German Dictionary, $1.00. *Physics:* Gage's Introduction to Physical Science, $1.00. *Drawing:* Blank Drawing Book (manilla paper).

*Recommended for Purchase.

BUSINESS COURSE.—*Book-keeping:* Goodwin's, $1.80. *English:* Pamphlets in English Classic Series. *Shorthand:* Dement's Pitmanic Manual, $1.40. *Commercial Law:* S. S. Clarke's Text-Book, $1.10. *Commercial Geography:* Tilden's, $1.00.

IN THE THIRD-YEAR CLASS.

English: Chaucer, Milton, Shakespeare, Hudson or Rolfe edition. *Trigonometry and Surveying:* Wentworth's (with tables) $1.30. *Mechanics:* Lodge's, $1.20. (Van Nostrand Co.). *Physics:* Thompson's Elements of Electricity, $1.35. *Latin:* Virgil's Æneid (Greenough's edition preferred), $1.70. Select Orations of Cicero (Allen & Greenough's new edition preferred), $1.25. Collar's Latin Prose Composition, $1.00. *German:* Geschichte der deutschen Litteratur, 75 cts. Goethe's Meisterwerke, $1.50. *Greek:* Goodwin's Greek Grammar, $1.50. Goodwin's Xenophon's Anabasis, $1.50. *Botany:* Gray's Lessons and Manual, $2.25. *Chemistry:* Eliot and Storer's Manual, $1.15. *Mineralogy:* Crosby's Tables, $1.35. *Civil Government:* Fiske's Civil Government in the U. S., $1.00. *Drawing:* Blank Drawing Book (manilla paper).

IN THE FOURTH-YEAR CLASS.

English: (References may be procured as needed). *Latin:* Virgil's Æneid, The Eclogues (any edition). *German:* Goethe's Meisterwerke, $1.50. *Greek:* Seymour's Homer's Iliad, $1.25. Goodwin's Greek Grammar, $1.50. *History:* Myer's General History, $1.50. *Botany:* Bower's Practical Botany, $2.60. *Geology:* Le Conte's Compend, $1.20.

COURSES OF STUDY OUTLINED.

YEAR.	ACADEMIC.	SCIENTIFIC.
First.	English. History. Algebra. Latin. Zoölogy.	English. History. Algebra. German. Zoölogy.
Second.	English and English History. *Greek.* Geometry. Latin. Physics or Chemistry.	English and English History. Geometry. German. Physics or Chemistry.
Third.	*Trig'y* and *Surveying* or *History.* Latin. English. German. *Greek.* *Botany* or *Chemistry* and *Mineralogy*, or *Advanced Physics*.	*Trig'y* and *Surveying* or *History.* German. English. *Botany* or *Chemistry* and *Mineralogy*, or *Advanced Physics*.
Fourth.	Latin. English. *Advanced Botany* or *Chemistry* or *Physics*. *Greek.* Geology. History. *Analytical Geometry* and *College Algebra*. *Political Economy*.	German. English. *Advanced Botany* or *Chemistry* or *Physics*. Geology. History. *Analytical Geometry* and *College Algebra*. *Political Economy*.

(a.) Elective studies are printed in italics; all others are prescribed.
(b.) General exercises in Drawing are required in all the courses; a general exercise in Music is optional, except for Normal School candidates, for whom it is prescribed.
(c.) Military drill will be conducted under the same regulations as during the past year.
(d.) Manual training for pupils of both sexes throughout each course is optional.
(e.) Not more than four studies may be pursued at one time.
(f.) Candidates for diplomas must pursue all the prescribed studies and four studies in the third and fourth years; students who, from any cause, fail to meet this requirement, are enrolled as "unclassified" and cannot graduate until the prescribed work is satisfactorily made up.
(g.) Pupils who desire to prepare for college can make special arrangements of their courses upon written application to the principal; this must be done by pupils of the second year who elect Greek.
(h.) Pupils who have satisfactorily completed the three years' course shall be entitled to a diploma, and those who have completed the advanced (or fourth year) course to an additional diploma.

BUSINESS HIGH SCHOOL.

BOOK-KEEPING.
FIRST YEAR.

Time, five hours a week—*One hundred and eighty hours*. Text-book, first two quarters, Bryant & Stratton's Common School, including single and double entry. Last two quarters, selected sets of practice exercises.

SECOND YEAR.

Time, five hours a week—*One hundred and eighty hours*. Goodwin's text-book. Banking, business practice, solution of book-keeping problems, preparation of sample sets.

BUSINESS ARITHMETIC.
FIRST YEAR.

Time, three hours a week—*One hundred and eight hours*. Text-book, Sadler's Inductive, with special attention to business problems.

SECOND YEAR.

Time, one hour a week—*Thirty-six hours*. Review of first year work, miscellaneous problems.

ENGLISH.
FIRST YEAR.

Time, four hours a week. Text-book, first three quarters, Lockwood's English. *One hundred and eight hours*. Fourth quarter, Eaton's Manual of Correspondence. *Thirty-six hours*.

SECOND YEAR.

Time, four hours a week. First quarter, review of grammar using Kerl's text-book. *Thirty-six hours*. Second and third quarters, critical reading of selected works. *Seventy-two hours*. Fourth quarter, review of the two years' work. *Thirty-six hours*.

SHORTHAND.
FIRST YEAR.

Time, three hours a week. Text-book, first three quarters, Barnes' Manual. *Eighty-one hours*. Fourth quarter, slow dictation and transcription on typewriter of notes. *Twenty-seven hours*.

SECOND YEAR.

Dictation and transcription of notes on the typewriter.

COMMERCIAL GEOGRAPHY.

SECOND YEAR.

Time, two hours a week. Text-book, Tilden's Commercial Geography. *Seventy-two hours.* Special attention is given to the United States.

COMMERCIAL LAW.

SECOND YEAR.

Time, two hours a week—*Seventy-two hours.* S. S. text-book. Clark's. General business law with special attention to commercial paper.

MECHANICAL DRAWING.

FIRST YEAR.

Time, two hours a week—*Seventy-two hours.* Geometric problems, machine drawing from models.

SECOND YEAR.

Time, two hours a week—*Seventy-two hours.* Advanced problems in orthographic projection, machine drawing, architectural drawing.

PENMANSHIP.

FIRST YEAR.

Time, two hours a week—*Seventy-two hours.* Particular attention is given to position and movement.

SPELLING.

FIRST YEAR.

Time, one hour a week—*Thirty-six hours.* Words frequently misspelled in business.

TYPEWRITING.

FIRST YEAR.

Time, three hours a week. Text book, first three quarters, Barnes' Manual. *Eighty-one hours.* Fourth quarter, transcription of shorthand notes. *Twenty-seven hours.*

SECOND YEAR.

Writing from dictation and transcription of shorthand notes. *One hundred and eight hours.*

PHYSICAL TRAINING.

Military drill twice a week for boys. *One hundred and forty-four hours.* This course is elective. Delsarte drill twice a week for all girls. *Seventy-two hours.*

NORMAL TRAINING SCHOOLS.

I. A review of each branch of study pursued in the elementary schools, for the purpose of making topical outlines, logically arranged.

II. Psychology and Pedagogics.

III. A study of each branch of education pursued in the elementary schools to determine the order of presentation of the various parts thereof, and the relative importance of each part.

IV. Methods of instruction and practice in teaching.

V. Preparation of lessons and larger units of work for criticism; oral and written criticisms of teaching and of prepared work.

VI. Special preparation in writing on blackboard and rapid sketching for illustration and representation.

VII. The preparation and care of appliances.

VIII. Hygiene of the school-room; physical care of the pupils.

IX. Educational literature, its value and use.

X. Lectures on moral training and example.

APPENDIXES.

APPENDIX A.

POSITION, MOVEMENT AND USE OF PENCIL.

Position:

The pupil should face the desk. The first position should be the one given in the health exercises as the upright sitting position. This should be maintained in all the movement drills. A slight inclination forward of the upper portion of the body will bring the eyes over the paper. The eyes should never be nearer the paper than is necessary to enable the pupil to see the lines distinctly. The teacher should carefully examine near-sighted pupils to ascertain the distance at which they can see clearly. The fingers of the right hand should rest lightly upon the paper or book which should be directly under the right hand and parallel with the edges of the desk.

Movement:

In all drill exercises the whole arm movement should be used. Pupils should not be permitted to limit movement to the muscles of the hand. The right hand should not rest on the desk.

In drawing horizontal lines the movement should be from left to right.

In drawing vertical lines it should be from the upper to the lower end of the line.

In drawing oblique lines it should usually be from the upper to the lower end.

The left hand parts and the upper portions of a figure should be sketched first.

Use of Pencil:

The pencil should be held from three to five inches from the point at an angle of about 40° with the paper. The fingers should be slightly curved—that is neither straight nor cramped. (The exercises that give strength and flexibility to the muscles of the hand should be used in this connection). The lead of the pencils should be blunt and rounded. A broad uniform grey line should be the result.

In drawing straight lines the pencil should be held at right angles to the direction in which the line is to be drawn.

In drill on the circle and the vertical ellipse the pencil should be kept in the position for drawing vertical lines; in the horizontal ellipse and oval, it should be kept in the position for drawing horizontal lines. In drill on compound curves the same rule should be followed. The curve should be thoroughly analyzed before attempting the movement. Many trial movements should be made before the line is drawn.

APPENDIX B.

MODELING IN CLAY.

Part I.

Materials—Moist clay, and a surface upon which to work (a slate, a board or a piece of enamelled leather).

SUGGESTIONS.

Care should be taken to keep the clay in good condition. When not in use it is best kept in an earthen jar covered with a wet cloth.

The children should not be allowed to fall into careless habits of handling the clay. They should not be allowed, therefore, to take the clay in their hands until they know definitely what they are to do with it.

In presenting a new form for study each child should, if possible, have upon his desk a model, that he may handle the object, as well as see the form. If a single model is used, it should be of sufficient size to be seen by all in the class.

It is necessary to give specific directions for making the forms, and to direct the movements of the children. These directions should be emphasized by the use of the clay in the hands of the teacher.

The Sphere:

Study the model by looking at it and by handling it.

The first year give about one cubic inch of clay to each child. Show the children how to form a ball of this clay with the fingers, not with the hands. Direct them to shape their clay in the same manner. They may then roll it lightly between the palms of the hands, the fingers being bent slightly backward. Ask them to name objects of similar form. Give the name *sphere*. Draw from the children the statement "The sphere will roll." Distribute pieces of clay to make spheres differing in size. Have these spheres arranged on the desk in different relations.

As the ideas of positions are developed, give the terms, corner, center, right, left, above, below, lower, upper, smaller, larger.

Some of the modifications of the sphere that are to be made are the apple, the peach, the orange, the tomato, grapes, nuts, and some simple pottery forms, as a ginger jar, a sugar bowl and a teapot. The children should be interested in procuring models to be imitated. They will then learn to see the sphere and its modifications, in nature and in art. When the sphere is to be changed to represent a modified form, it should be shaped entirely with the fingers, without rolling. The sphere is used during the first four years. Its size should be gradually increased from one inch in the first year to two inches in the fourth year.

The Cube:

This is made from the sphere by striking it gently on the slate, developing the six sides in succession. Much care will be necessary to produce square faces and sharp edges.

While modeling the cube, as the ideas of face, edge and corner are developed through the study of the model, the terms should be used by the teacher and by the children.

The cube should be modeled many times, that the children may be able to make it well, and that they may describe it well.

Terms—straight, edge, corner, face, flat, square, cube. Modifications of the cube are few. A box or a square ink-stand may be used, and in connection with the triangular prism, a toy house.

The Square Prism:

A curved oblong form should be made with the fingers as described in the directions for making a sphere. The square prism may be developed from this in the same manner as the cube is developed from the sphere. The form should be studied in a similar way. The pupils should be encouraged to discover the rectangular form in objects, some of which, should be modeled in clay; as boxes, books, bricks, bottles, etc.

The Triangular Prism:

This form should be developed in the same way as the foregoing prisms and lessons upon it should be given in a corresponding way. The right-angled triangular prism may be developed also from the square prism by cutting it diagonally.

The Hemisphere:

For this form the sphere is cut with a thread. Cups, bowls, hats, etc., based upon the hemisphere, should be modeled by the children. These should be modeled as solids.

The Cylinder:

This form is developed from the curved oblong form, which is rolled for the curved surface of the cylinder, the ends being flattened by striking, as in the cube. Many objects based on this form will be discovered, as bottles, jugs, rolling pins, pint cups, etc.

The Ellipsoid:

This form is shaped with the fingers, copying the model. The lemon, plum, potato, melon, should be modeled in this connection.

The Ovoid:

This form is shaped in the same way from the model. The pear, acorn, gourds and vases will illustrate this form.

The Cone:

This form is developed from the ovoid. The ovoid is shaped with the fingers, copying a model. It is then rolled for the curved surface, the weight of the palm being nearer the small end. The large end is flattened for the circular plane. Objects based on the cone should be modeled, as a flower pot, a cup, goblet or a vase.

The Square Pyramid:

This form may be developed from the cone, in the same manner as the cube is from the sphere. Paper weights and thermometers are often based upon this form. Monuments, church towers, and other architectural features may be observed, and the general contour and more prominent details represented from memory, that the children may be led to observe the form in architecture and elsewhere.

Opportunity should be given to the children to model in clay, forms which they have observed, that a closer observation may be encouraged. The use made of all these geometric forms on gate posts and fences is a good subject for observation. The teacher should note all applications of these forms in the school building and in other buildings in the immediate neighborhood, and lead the children to look for them.

The same geometric forms are used in the third and fourth years that are used in the first and second. The size alone varies. The shortest diameter of all geometric forms used in the fourth year should be two inches. Vases and other forms of pottery should be the principal objects used for models in the fourth year. A slate pencil may be used to support the clay while building up these forms. The accessories as handles, etc., should be carefully modeled (not rolled) and thoroughly incorporated with the mass of clay. It is better to avoid objects having very slender handles.

LANGUAGE.

While doing this work the children may be led to ask and answer questions relative to the material they use, the objects they represent, the properties of these objects, and the processes by which the modeling is done. Let this language work be simple and natural, adhering at the same time to a logical arrangement of thought. Avoid all carelessness of seeing, and the consequent loose description of what is seen.

PART II.

The modeling from the fifth to the eighth year inclusive is connected with the study of decoration, a change being made from modeling in the round to modeling in relief.

Before the pupils begin to model at least one lesson should be given in each grade with clay in the hands of the teacher showing the successive steps and the manner of handling the clay.

These steps are:
1 Shaping the plinth.
2 Blocking the general form, massing the clay to show the principal elevations and depressions.
3 Finishing with details of edges and surfaces.

In making the plinth the upper surface should be level but not smooth that the clay of the form may be thoroughly incorporated with that of the plinth. At first the modeling can be done with the fingers aided by a simple tool that the children themselves can shape from a wooden pen-holder or other bit of wood. For advanced work the pupil should have one or two of the tools used for modeling in clay; these cost about ten cents each and can be purchased at art stores.

The teacher should remember that this work is modeling, not casting in a mold.

All appliances which are calculated to accomplish results without thought must be avoided. The value of the work is in the process of thoughtfully evolving from the shapeless mass the desired form.

The surface of the finished model should show texture. Smoothing and polishing destroy this beauty.

In using natural leaves as models a careful selection should be made of those that retain their form and that give opportunity for surface modeling. The ivy and magnolia have been suggested in this course of study because they possess these qualities and also because they can be easily procured in quantities in this vicinity. The calla, begonias and a few of the geraniums also furnish good subjects. In advanced work when a branch with several leaves is taken as a subject greater variety is possible. In seventh and eighth grades individual work may be done taking for models fruits, shells, etc. These may be modeled in the round, or in high relief. The teacher having explained the difference between these modes of treatment the pupil should decide which he will adopt. If the form is to be modeled in the round, no plinth should be made; if in relief the forms should be built up from the plinth, and thoroughly incorporated with it, care being taken in the undercutting.

Every school should possess at least one good example in terra cotta or plaster of each kind of work expected from the pupils of the grade. These should be carefully studied.

Historic ornament should be modeled from examples in relief.

Cutting an ornament in clay has some advantages over modeling, one of which is that it can be executed from outline studies either from those supplied in the drawing book or from other good examples drawn on the blackboard.

If the subject is well chosen the flat treatment is pleasing. This is often employed in ornamentation. Directions: Mould and cut to shape a plinth of suitable size. A plinth whose length is about five inches should be one inch thick; if larger the thickness should be greater. The clay for this should be thoroughly worked and the surface of the plinth made smooth and even. When partially dry the outline may be drawn upon it and the clay cut away leaving the pattern in relief. It should be cut to a depth ranging from 1-16 to ½ inch according to the character of the subject. Pupils may reproduce their designs for tiles and borders in this way. If the clay is not too dry the cutting can be done with a wooden tool by sharpening a cylindrical piece of wood to an edge or it can be done with a steel eraser.

If the pattern is to be incised, the reverse of this process is necessary, that is, the pattern is cut away leaving the surrounding surface raised. Attention should be called to the difference in treatment and to the kinds of design best suited to each process. Designs for cutting in clay should be made with the intention of adapting them to one or the other process.

APPENDIX C.

TABLET AND STICK LAYING.

Materials—Sticks of different lengths and colors.

Tablets:

In the construction of a geometric form use but one color. Train the child to understand that form is independent of size, by using sticks of different lengths for the construction of the same form. Require the children to select for themselves the size, form and color required.

Directions should sometimes be given orally and sometimes by drawings on the blackboard.

In the beginning of this work special attention should be given to the position of the body, hand, paper and pencil while drawing, that the good effects of the drills given in the first of the year may not be lost.

In this course special attention should be given to the correct representation of form by drawing, but language should never be neglected. All new words used in conducting the various exercises should be written on the blackboard and used in sentences.

FIRST YEAR.

Position:

Each child is given one long stick. It is held in a vertical position.

The term vertical is given. Other objects, as rulers, pencils and |paper-folders, are held in vertical positions. Teacher illustrates vertical position by pictures drawn on the board.

Edges in the room that are vertical are observed. The child is directed to place his stick on his desk, the ends pointing to the back and front of the desk respectively. This should be drawn full length.

A number of sticks are selected, and the child is directed to place them in like positions in a row on the upper part of the desk, then by spacing to place them in groups of three. The arrangements should be drawn on paper by the children; the length of the lines on paper should correspond with the length of the sticks.

Other grouping of the sticks should be suggested by the teacher or invented by the child, as alternate groups of three and two, four and two, etc., with different spacings. Drawings of these should be made, special attention being given to ideas of length, and to spacing, both in the stick laying and in the drawing.

All drawings must be made free-hand.

All constructions which are to be represented by drawings should be placed in the upper left-hand corner of the desk.

Expressions of opinion as to which arrangements are most pleasing should be drawn from the children. Some of the best arrangements should be represented by drawing on the blackboard.

The children should represent by drawings, objects involving vertical lines; as a ruler, a pencil, a cane, or a paper-folder.

Familiar forms that are usually vertical in position, as trees, lamp-posts, telegraph poles, etc., may be observed, and drawings of some of them may be made from memory.

The ideas of the horizontal and oblique positions should be developed in a similar manner.

Some ornamental combinations may be placed on the board as the Greek fret, and the zigzag.

Also some suggestions of familiar forms as the side of a table and a chair, the roof of a house, a ladder, fences, railings, etc.

These should first be made with sticks, then should be represented by drawings. The children should be encouraged to invent and remember other forms which are to be constructed and represented in a similar way.

The Square:

The idea of the square has been developed from the side of the cube.

Place a square tablet upon the desk. Children place around this sticks of suitable length. They should then be asked to make the shape of the square with sticks of different lengths.

The children should represent their squares by drawings of the same size as the constructions.

Another exercise should be the construction of the square in other positions.

Ornamental forms composed of squares should be invented, constructed, and represented by drawings.

These should first be laid with tablets, and afterwards with sticks. The circular tablets may be used in alternation with the right-lined forms. Sticks for border lines will add to the beauty of the designs.

Various square forms should be recalled to memory by the children, and efforts should be made to represent them by drawings.

Such forms may be found in small mirrors, picture frames, checkerboards, some window-panes, books, tiles, etc. Without mentioning these, ask the children to seek this form in objects at home and in the street, to discover how many things they can find that are square.

The idea of the rectangular oblong and of the right-angled triangle should be developed in a similar manner.

Parallel Lines and Angles:

Find in the square and oblong tablet edges that do not meet.
Find edges that do meet.
Gives terms *parallel* and *angle*.
Place sticks in similar positions.

Find parallel egdes, and edges at angles in the room and in various objects. Illustrate angles by pictures drawn on the board. Children draw pictures illustrating angles.

Right Angles:

Show the corner of the square.
Construct the right angle with sticks in every possible position.
Find how many right angles can be made with two sticks, with three, with four.
Use sticks of different lengths.
Draw all these forms, preserving the proper size.
Find these angles in the room and in various objects.
Draw as many of these objects as possible.
The letters of the alphabet containing right angles are good subjects for construction and drawing.
The idea of the acute and obtuse angles should be developed in a similar manner, using the triangular tablet.
Little twigs branching in various directions may be selected and used as objects for representation while teaching angles.
Divisions of lines should be taught with the sticks by using a two-inch stick, and forming another with two one-inch sticks, using a three-inch stick and forming another of one-inch sticks, etc. The first line may be drawn and points placed as indicated in the second constructed line.

Rhomb:

Each child selects four three-inch sticks.
Draw on the blackboard a square on its diameters, a square on its diagonals, and a rhomb.
Children observe the points of difference and the points of resemblance between the figures.
Give the name.
Children construct the rhomb with sticks; observe or recall anything that may be of this shape.
They represent the form by a drawing.
The size of the drawing should be the same as that of the form constructed by the sticks.

Distribute sticks of different sizes. The children construct rhombs and represent them by drawings, adhering as before, to the size of the construction.

Give a number of sticks to each child. Draw on the board an ornamental border of rhombs.

Let the children construct it with sticks.

Let them represent it by drawings.

Let them invent other arrangements for borders with sticks and draw them. Suggest that they look at the borders of their handkerchiefs. Lead the children in the same way to construct and draw ornamental forms composed of rhombs grouped around a center, a rhomb in an oblong, etc.

In presenting these subjects for drawing give directions for the best methods of constructing the drawings (construction lines to be erased), the proper division of lines, etc.; the lines should never be ruled.

The Rhomboid:

The idea of this form should be developed in a manner similar to that for the development of the rhomb.

The child should be led to observe the points of resemblance and difference between the oblong and the rhomboid, and between the rhomb and the rhomboid.

Invent, construct, represent by drawing.

Observe and represent forms based on the rhomboid. For the construction of ornamental forms care should be taken that sticks of a suitable length are selected. Experiments in construction and invention should be made by the teacher before giving the lessons.

The Trapezoid:

The idea of this form should be developed in a manner similar to that for the development of the rhomboid.

The equilateral and isosceles triangles should be treated in a similar manner.

The tablets, ellipses, ovals and triangles, with sticks for enclosing lines will furnish a great variety of ornamental forms and should be freely used in inventive arrangements.

APPENDIX D.

PAPER FOLDING.

Materials:

Four-inch squares of paper, three tints of each color.

See that each child is provided with material.

See that the children use the material with care, neatness and accuracy.

Let the representation go hand in hand with the folding, the making of forms.

Develop the vocabulary of form naturally; that is, by a consistent use of the terms involved while discovering, making and representing form. Let the teacher use the necessary terms, write them on the board, then lead the children to recognize them and to use them in connection with their work.

Combine tints of one color using only two tints in any arrangement. In borders use but one tint.

Fold the geometric form in the standard red, blue or yellow.

Teach color in connection with the folding as indicated in the course of study.

DIRECTIONS.

The Square:

Place a square of paper on each desk; lead pupils to state that their papers differ in color; that their papers are alike in shape, size and material; that each paper has four edges and four corners.

Let the pupils show the right edge, the left edge, the front (lower or nearer) edge, the upper or back edge, the nearer right corner, the farther right corner.

Let the pupils place the squares on their desk, having the edges parallel with the edges of their desks, the color side down.

Let each pupil lift the front edge and lay it on the back edge. Ask "Which is longer?" Fold the paper; open it; fold the left edge on the right edge.

Let the pupils compare the front edge and the back edge with the right edge.

Lead them to state that the edges are equal. Lead them to see that the corners are right angled, by placing two sticks as in stick-laying.

Lead the pupils to find the lines which connect the left edge with the right edge; the upper edge with the lower edge.

Lead them to find where these lines cross. Give the term *diameter*. Let them fold from the lower left hand corner to the upper right hand corner, and unfold; then from the lower right to the upper left corner, and unfold.

Let the pupils show the lines that connect the right back corner and the left front corner; the left back corner and the right front corner.

Give the term *diagonal*.

Let them find the exact size of the square.

Lead the children to discover familiar objects based on the square, such as picture-frames, books, square envelopes, napkins, handkerchiefs, banners, hand-bags, school-bags, the gable ends of toy houses.

Let the pupils represent by drawings the square and familiar objects based on the square.

Let the children place the square on the desk, having a diagonal vertical to the front edge of the desk. Show the center of the square, the back corner, the right corner, the left corner. Fold the back corner to the center; the front corner to the center; the left corner and the right corner to the center.

Do not let the children change the position of the paper.

· Let them compare the folded forms with the four-inch square.

Let them turn the square over, fold the farther left corner and the nearer right corner to the center; fold the nearer left corner and the farther right corner to the center.

Always fold opposite corners to keep the form symmetrical.

Compare the square now with the four-inch square. (One-fourth of its size).

Divide four-inch squares into fourths.

Place two squares of one tint side by side, the edges parallel with the edges of the desks.

Move the right one back, so that only the corners touch.

Fill the spaces with squares of another tint.

Ask "What have you done?" "How many small squares have you?" "How many squares have you that are alike?" "How many pairs of squares?"

Let the pupils arrange the squares differently. Let the pupils represent some of these combinations by drawings.

The Oblong Rectangle:

Place a square of paper on the desk, the edges parallel with the edges of the desk. Fold the front edge to meet the back edge. Compare the edges and angles with those of the square. Give the term *oblong*.

Lead the children to discover familiar objects based on the oblong, such as slates, book-covers, envelopes, picture-frames, flags, banners, hand-bags, school-bags, the sides of boxes, a toy washboard, a toy ladder, the side of a toy house, dominoes, pocket-books and ornamental forms, such as crosses.

Let them represent, by drawings, the geometric form and the forms based on it.

Let them divide four-inch squares, fold and arrange them in different ways.

Let the pupils represent some of these combinations by drawings.

The Triangle—right-angled:

Place the squares on the desks, having the diagonals perpendicular to the edges of the desk.

Fold the front corner to meet the back corner.

Ask questions about the folded form as follows: "How many sides has it?" "How many corners or angles has it?" "How many equal sides has it?" Let the children show the longest side. Give the term *triangle*.

Lead them to discover familiar objects based on the triangle, such as handkerchiefs and napkins folded in triangular forms, children's soldier caps, picture cards, triangular fans.

Let them represent the triangle and familiar objects based on it. Divide a square and make four smaller triangles; arrange them in a border and around a center.

Let them combine triangles and squares.

SECOND YEAR.

Trapezoid:

Fold the right-angled triangle. Place it with the long edge vertical to the front edge of the desk, and on the right. Fold the left corner to meet the middle of the long side.
Compare edges, find angles and give name.
Represent the form by a drawing. Discover familiar forms based on the trapezoid.
Divide the square into fourths.
Make a trapezoid of each.
Place two of them with their small straight sides together.
Move the upper one back.
Place the other two, one at the right and one at the left, so that the slanting edges will meet the slanting edges of those first placed.
Invent other arrangements.
Represent, by drawings, objects based on the trapezoid; a boat, a soldier's paper cap, etc.
Observe forms in furniture and buildings that are modifications of the trapezoid, etc., and represent them from memory.
Fold a trapezoid as before.
Fold the sharp corner to meet the center of the long side.
Compare angles and sides. Show that it has two parallel sides but is a trapezoid.
Represent the form by a drawing.
Make designs using these.
Represent some of these combinations. Represent, by drawings, objects that are modifications of this form, as a shoe.
Observe in furniture and buildings such forms, and draw them from memory.
Fold a right-angled triangle. Place it with one short side parallel with the front of the desk and the other at the right. Fold lower left corner to meet the middle of right side. Lead the children to count the sides, to see that no two sides are equal; that no two sides are parallel. Give name trapezium. Ask the children to see if they can find any form that has four sides, no two of which are equal or parallel.

Triangle—acute isosceles:

Place squares on the desks, having the diagonals perpendicular to the edges of the desks. Fold right corner to meet left corner. Unfold. Fold right front edge to meet the diagonal. Fold the left front edge to meet the diagonal. Turn the square corner over as far as possible.

Compare edges as before. Discover and name the angles by the use of sticks or comparison with the corners of a square.

Represent the form by drawing.

Lead pupils to make designs and to represent some of the best by drawings.

Observe and draw from memory a church steeple or any other similar form.

Triangle—right scalene:

Fold an acute isosceles triangle.
Fold the long edges together.
Compare edges and find angles as before.

The Rhomboid:

Place squares on the desks (edges parallel with edges of desks).
Fold the back left corner to meet front right corner.
Unfold.
Fold the front edge to lie on the diagonal.
Fold the back edge to lie on the diagonal.

The Long Rhombus:

Fold a rhomboid. Place long edges parallel with front edge of desk; fold left edge to lie on the diagonal. Fold right edge to lie on the diagonal.

The Kite Pentagon:

Fold a rhombus.
Fold one sharp corner to meet the center.
Develop the lessons on each of these forms as has been suggested in the lessons given on other forms.

PAPER-CUTTING AND PASTING.

The paper-cutting for the third and fourth years is connected with the subject of decorative design.

The Purposes of this Work are:

To cultivate the taste of the children in making combinations in form and color.

To teach them the laws of symmetry and of adaptation to space.

To lead them to see the value of the geometric basis in ornament.

To suggest to them the use that may be made of natural forms.

The materials required for this work are scissors for cutting, good mucilage, prepared paste or Page's glue, and three tints each of colored paper.

DIRECTIONS.

In each combination use two or three tints of one color; do not combine the colors.

The first lesson given relates to units and their modifications.

1. Let the children divide a square of paper into four squares and fold each into the kite-shaped form by placing the corners of the squares next to them, folding for the diagonals, unfolding and then folding the lower right and left edges on the diagonals. Let them arrange these four units horizontally to form borders. Give them squares and let them arrange the forms on the diagonals. Give the term "unit of design." Let the children fold the unit on its diameter developing the idea of symmetry. Give terms axis, symmetrical unit.

2. Distribute squares of paper and dictate the drawing of a large unit as follows: Place paper, color side down, with corner next to the edge of the desk; fold right corner to left corner; open; divide this diagonal into three equal parts. Through the upper point of division draw a horizontal line touching the sides of the square; connect the ends of this line with the lower end of the diagonal; mark off one-fourth of an inch on the upper end of the diagonal; from this point draw lines parallel with the upper sides of the square to meet the long sides of the unit.

Draw this figure on the board and show some ways in which it may be modified by curves; let the children modify their units in similar ways and cut them.

Teach the children to designate their colors as, (name of color), light, lighter; example—olive, light olive, lighter olive.

3. Divide the school into sections of two rows each. Give two squares of paper to each child, giving to each section a different color, and to each of the two rows of a section a different combination of tints. Let each child divide one of the two squares into four squares as before; on one of these let him draw the kite-shaped unit, as in the former lesson. Modify and cut it as before. Use it as a pattern for cutting the remaining units. Arrange these units on the diagonals of the entire square. With a small quantity of the mucilage fasten these units at the center. Teach the children to be neat in the use of mucilage.

4. Divide a number of the remaining papers of each color in the possession of the teacher into nine squares each. Give three of these to each child so that each will have a complement of tints. Draw a form on the board similar to that the children have arranged. Lead them to see that it requires something more to complete it; that it requires something to unite the parts and to give strength to the construction. Draw different centers; lead the children to see that to keep the form symmetrical the shape of the central form must be a square or a circle or some symmetrical modification of these forms; that if a square or a modification of it is chosen, it may be so placed that its diagonals will coincide either with the diagonals or the diameters of the large square. Let the children cut three centers, select the most pleasing and paste it. In later lessons they may be shown how units may be cut so that a simple underlying form will give the strength and unity now obtained by this center form.

The second geometric form used is the oblong. In this form and in the rhomb the principal idea developed is that a change in the proportions of the unit is often necessary to adapt it to the space it is to occupy. Children may make oblongs from the squares by cutting off from them strips one-third the width of the square. Draw an oblong on the board; call attention to the spaces to be filled; give the technical term field. Show, by drawing, how the proportions of the unit may be changed to suit the field. Children draw diameters on the back of the oblong from which the units are to be cut, and draw, cut and paste the units as before. Distribute small oblongs, the diameters of which should be one-third of the diameter of the large oblong, and show that some modification of this form is necessary to make a symmetrical center. It is better to use the simple kite-shaped unit in the first lesson showing changes in proportions. In subsequent lessons the units may be modified both in form and proportion.

The triangle is the remaining geometric form used in the third year. Borders should be made of simple units arranged horizontally and vertically. Strive first to lead the children to an appreciation of the beauty that may be obtained by repetition of a simple form of good proportions, especially when aided by harmonious arrangement of color. When simple units are modified the attention of the children should be called to the value of the intervening spaces; show that the unit is not good if in the repetition the intervening space is not of pleasing form and proportion. Borders may be made of two tints, one for the unit of design the other for the background, or of one tint on a background of neutral grey.

The pentagon, hexagon and octagon used in the fourth year are new to the children. Their construction should be carefully taught in the folding and cutting of the first pattern. The construction of the five and six pointed star from the pentagon and hexagon should be taught. The units designed for this radiating form should be suggested by the petals of flowers or by leaves. Lead the children to see the principle of these radiating forms in flowers and carefully explain how these natural forms are adapted to the perfect symmetry and simplicity necessary in the art form. This form in art is called a rosette. In the fourth year suggestions for units may be obtained from the shapes of leaves and from the petals of flowers.

In the fifth grade colored paper is one of the materials suggested for the expression of the children's ideas of design. The surface patterns and the borders designed in this grade are very beautiful when executed in the tints of gray and brown provided for the purpose.

RULES

OF THE

Public Schools of the District of Columbia.

ADMISSION OF PUPILS.

1. Separate schools for White children and for Colored children shall be provided in accordance with existing laws.

2. The number of teachers appointed for each division shall not be less than one for each fifty pupils of the average enrollment.

3. All children between the ages of six and seventeen years, inclusive, whose parents are residents of the District of Columbia, shall be entitled to admission into such schools within the division in which they reside for which on examination they may be found qualified: *Provided*, That no child shall be admitted who shall not have been duly vaccinated or otherwise protected from small-pox; nor shall any child be admitted while suffering from, or liable to spread, any contagious disease. A certificate of the attending physician shall in such cases be required to admit or re-admit to school.

4. Applications for admission into City schools shall be made to the principal teachers in the respective school buildings. Applicants, if found qualified, shall have precedence in the order in which they present themselves at the schools to which they are assigned.

5. At the commencement of each school year the order of admission of pupils shall be as follows:

I. The pupils who were such at the [close of the last year: *Provided*, That they return on the first school day of the school year.

II. Pupils transferred in due form from other schools, who must first have been entered on their rolls.

III. Applicants in the order of presenting themselves.

In cases of sickness, or necessary absence from the District, the seats of pupils of the first of the above classes shall be reserved until the beginning of the fourth school day of the school year: *Provided*, that a satisfactory representation be made to the teacher prior to the time named above.

6. Promotions to a higher grade shall be made at the opening of the schools in September, and at no other time, except by special permission from the Superintendent; and those only shall be promoted whose attendance, conduct, and improvement shall have been satisfactory.

7. No pupil shall be received from one school into another without a transfer ticket, a certificate of honorable dismission, or satisfactory reason assigned for leaving the other; and no pupil shall be transferred from a school in one division into one of another, unless by written consent of the Local Committee of each division.

MEMBERSHIP OF PUPILS.

8. When pupils have been admitted into school their membership continues during the school age, unless terminated in the following ways:

I. A pupil may withdraw from school on notice from the parent or guardian to the teacher. The notice should be given at the time of leaving; if not, the name of the pupil must be continued on the roll and the absence must be marked on the record-book until such notice is received by the teacher: *Provided*, That the absence shall not extend beyond three successive school days; if no notice is received and the pupil does not return at the *beginning* of the fourth successive school day, the membership shall terminate and the seat shall be marked forfeited.

II. Pupils shall forfeit their seats by absence from school for more than three successive school days *for any cause*, whether with leave or without, whether with intention of returning or not, and whether the absence be occasioned by sickness, *suspension*, or other causes; and in all such cases if the pupil do not return at the *beginning* of the fourth successive school day, the membership shall terminate and the seat shall be marked forfeited. On returning, those who may have been detained by sickness shall have preference in admittance to school, and shall be readmitted by the teacher. Pupils may forfeit their seats, also, by failing to return to school or to make the required representation to the teacher on the first school day of the school year.

III. A pupil may be dismissed by order of the Supervising Principal, Superintendent, Local Committee, or Board.

IV. A pupil may be transferred; and a transfer terminates the membership of a pupil in the particular school or class from which the transfer is made.

V. For the purpose contemplated in this rule any pupil shall be considered as absent whose attendance shall not continue for at least one-half of the regular school session of the half day.

At the request of parents or guardians teachers shall excuse pupils from attendance at school on school days observed as holy days by the denomination to which the parents or guardians belong. All absence from school on school days must be duly recorded in the record-books and reported; but absence excused by teachers for the reason given above shall not affect the membership of pupils or any award made for attendance.

DUTIES OF PUPILS.

9. Good order and propriety of deportment, not only during school hours, but in coming to and going from school, and cleanliness in person and attire, are required from pupils. They are required to keep all books clean, and the contents of desks neatly arranged; to enter and leave the room in a respectful manner and without noise; and to quit the neighborhood of the school in a quiet and orderly manner immediately on being dismissed.

10. No pupil shall mark, cut, scratch, chalk, or otherwise disfigure or injure any portion of the school building or anything connected with it; use tobacco in any form; use any profane or indelicate language; throw stones or other missiles; annoy or maltreat others; or do anything that may disturb the neighborhood or the school. Any damage done to the school building, premises or furniture, must be repaired at the expense of the offender.

11. The following are sufficient grounds, severally, for the suspension of a pupil from the privileges of a school by the teacher, or for dismissal by the Supervising Principal, Superintendent, or Local Committee, viz:

Immoral conduct; violent or pointed opposition to authority in any particular instance; persistent disobedience or disorder; absence for four half days in any month, unless caused by personal sickness or by the presence of a contagious disease in the family, or when authorized in writing by a Local Committee or by the Superintendent (of which the teacher must be informed before the expiration of the fourth half day): *Provided*, That parents or guardians shall be notified immediately when their children have been absent two half days in any month; habitual tardiness, or uncleanliness of person or clothes, or neglect on the part of the parent or guardian to furnish the necessary school books, unless satisfactorily explained.

The teacher shall immediately notify the parent or guardian in every case of dismissal, and the Supervising Principal, Superintendent, or Local Committee, as well as the parent or guardian, in every case of suspension, with the reason therefor.

12. Any pupil suspended under the foregoing rule who shall express to the teacher regret for his or her misconduct, and shall give promise of amendment, shall, with the consent of the Supervising Principal, Superintendent, or Local Committee, be restored; but not otherwise.

Every Public School pupil of the District who, after a fair hearing, shall be shown to have carried upon any Public School premises, or to have had in possession while going to or returning from school, any pistol or other firearm, shall be summarily expelled from the Public Schools, and shall not be reinstated during the then pending school year.

• 13. No pupil who has been absent or appears after the opening of the school shall be admitted without a satisfactory excuse from the parent or guardian for the absence or tardiness or without satisfactory explanation for the remissness. No pupil shall be allowed to be absent from school during the regular sessions to take music, drawing, dancing or other lessons; and no pupil shall be allowed to depart before the appointed hour of leaving school, except in case of sickness or on some pressing emergency, and the teacher in every case shall be the judge of the sufficiency of the excuse. The teacher may require excuses to be made in writing, and all notes of excuse shall be preserved until the close of the school year.

14. Not more than three lessons may be assigned daily to be studied at home by pupils above the fifth grade.

15. Pupils whose parents or guardians are in indigent circumstances may obtain a loan of books and other articles required for their use in the school on a written application approved by the teacher of the school and by the Supervising Principal or a Local Committee, in such form as shall be prescribed by the Board; but in all cases such books shall be returned whenever the pupil shall leave the school. If they shall not be returned by the pupil, the teacher shall report the fact to the Supervising Principal or Superintendent, and the pupil shall not be permitted again to enter any Public School in the District.

TEACHERS.

16. Teachers' certificates shall be issued in five classes as follows, commencing with the lowest:

The First-Class Certificate shall be sufficient evidence of the scholastic qualifications required for temporary appointment as teacher and as substitute teacher; the Second-Class Certificate for teaching in any school from the First Grade to the Third Grade, inclusive; the Third-Class Certificate in any school from the First Grade to the Fifth Grade, inclusive; the Fourth-Class Certificate in any school from the First Grade to the Seventh Grade, inclusive; the Fifth-Class Certificate in any school from the First Grade to the Eighth Grade, inclusive; and for all other positions the examinations and certificates shall be special.

17. Teachers of schools of any grade must be not less than eighteen years of age.

18. No person shall be appointed teacher of any school who shall not have received from the Committee on Teachers and Janitors the certificate required for the grade of the school to which appointed: *Provided, however*, that in cases where vacancies exist for which qualified teachers under this rule cannot be obtained, such vacancies may be otherwise temporarily filled until a properly qualified teacher is available, and no longer; and, *provided further*, that all appointments of substitutes and temporary teachers shall be made from certificate holders, and in the order of excellence as determined by the examination, so long as there shall be unemployed holders of certificates available for the purpose.

Graduates of the Washington Normal School and of the Normal School of the Seventh and Eighth divisions shall be assigned to duty as teachers, in the order of their standing and excellence, as shown by the certificates of the respective principals.

Graduates of other approved Normal Schools shall stand upon an equal footing with certificate holders, and may be nominated instead of the highest certificate holder in the discretion of the Local Committee. Any graduate of the Washington Normal School or of the Normal School of the Seventh and Eighth divisions who shall not be assigned to duty within the school year succeeding graduation, shall stand on an equal footing with graduates of other approved Normal Schools.

No teacher shall engage in any business, trade, or occupation independent of the Public Schools without having first obtained the consent of this Board.

19. All appointments of teachers shall be for the remainder of the school year in which they take effect, unless previously otherwise ordered, but teachers at any time may be assigned or transferred to such schools as the Local Committee may designate or may be removed by the Board for incompetency, immorality, absence from duty, intoxication, or other violation of the rules.

Should a female teacher marry, her place shall thereupon become vacant, but such marriage shall not operate as a bar to her re-appointment, with the approval of this Board.

20. The salaries of all teachers duly elected, whose services shall begin with the school year, and who shall perform their duties, shall begin on the first day of September, and shall be paid in ten equal monthly instalments, the first to be made on the first of October, or as near that date as practicable. The salaries of other teachers shall begin when they enter upon duties. The pay for a school day shall be the thirtieth part of the tenth part of the annual salary of the teacher. Any teacher who shall be absent from duty without leave granted by the Superintendent, may be suspended by the Local Committee and dismissed by the Board. The suspension from duty of any teacher upon charges involving the penalty of removal shall involve cessation of pay or compensation from the date

of suspension when the removal is subsequently ordered upon such charges. Teachers who desire to relinquish their positions during the school year shall apply, through the Local Committee, to the Committee on Teachers and Janitors, submitting in writing their reasons therefor. Teachers abandoning their positions without consent of the Committee on Teachers and Janitors, are subject to dismissal and shall forfeit all pay due them.

DUTIES OF TEACHERS.

21. Teachers are required to be at their school-rooms and open the same for the admission of pupils at least fifteen minutes before the time appointed for the opening of the school. Teachers who shall be either tardy or absent shall report the fact on the monthly report and assign the reason therefor.

22. They shall not be absent from school at any time during the school year, except in cases of sickness, the presence of contagious disease in the family or other pressing emergency, notice of which shall be forthwith communicated to the Supervising Principal, Superintendent, or Local Committee; but the Superintendent may permit them to be absent for the purpose of visiting other schools, not exceeding two school days in any one year.

Leave of absence shall not be granted to a teacher for a longer time than three months, and then without pay : *Provided*, That on the recommendation of the local trustee a leave of absence may be renewed or extended for an additional term or terms of months: *Provided further*, That no leave shall be granted to a teacher who seeks such leave to engage in another occupation for pay or profit.

The resignation of a teacher, brought about by the payment of money to the resigning teacher by a Normal graduate or any other applicant, to obtain the position thus vacated, shall be deemed a violation of the rules of this board, and shall forever disqualify the applicant so offending for appointment as a teacher, and the teacher encouraging the same by receiving compensation shall not be permitted to resign, but shall be dismissed.

23. They shall attend all meetings to which they are called and all special classes organized for their instruction and improvement by the Superintendent of the Board, and in case of failure to do so they shall furnish to the Superintendent a statement in writing of the reason therefor.

24. They shall keep record-books, complete the entries in them each day before leaving the school-room, and make such reports as shall be required by the Board, and they shall not be entitled to pay or re-election until they shall have complied with this rule. Immediately after the closing of the schools they shall deposit their record-books in the office of the Superintendent, taking care to make and retain in their desks a list of the names of the pupils on the rolls at the close of the year.

25. The necessary stationery, blanks, and supplies for Public School purposes shall be furnished on requisition of the teacher.

26. The teacher of each school shall prepare and keep in his or her desk, for inspection, a programme of the exercises of each day during the week, specifying the length of time devoted to each study and recitation.

Teachers shall, at the beginning of the school year, report in writing to the Secretary of the School Board and to the Supervising Principal of the division in which they are employed, their residence—street and number; and any changes of residence during the year shall be reported, and the Secretary of the Board and the Supervising Principals shall keep a record of the same in their offices.

27. Teachers shall not engage, during school hours in reading, writing letters, conversation, or other occupations which are irrelevant to their duties as teachers. The use of tobacco, in or about the school building, is prohibited.

28. They shall prevent, as far as possible, the pupils from gathering on the school premises before the hours for opening the school-rooms; supervise their schools during the recesses; require the pupils to leave the premises immediately after the close of school; and, if the janitor is not present and in charge, see that the doors of the school-houses and other houses attached thereto are locked and the windows shut and fastened every day after the close of school.

29. They shall see to the safe-keeping and protection of furniture, apparatus, houses, fences, trees, shrubbery, fuel, and all other property of the schools. They shall maintain the strictest cleanliness in the schoolhouses and outhouses, and to this end they shall make frequent personal inspections of the buildings and grounds, respectively, under their charge, and maintain a strict supervision of their janitors. They shall promptly inform the Supervising Principal or the Local Committee whenever they find any loss of damage to have occurred, any repairs needed, or any other matter requiring his attention. At the close of each school year they shall return to the Supervising Principal all books and other articles loaned to indigent pupils.

30. It shall be the duty of the principal teacher in each building to place the school of a teacher, absent without having given one day's notice, promptly under a monitor, and to notify the Supervising Principal, to see that the rules relating to the deportment of pupils in the playrooms and halls, on the stairways and about the school buildings, on entering and leaving, and especially during the recesses, are enforced, and that all monthly reports and requisitions for supplies are made out promptly. For purposes of discipline the principal of every building may exercise all the powers and rights which pertain to teachers. Where several schools are grouped in one building each teacher shall co-operate

with the principal in maintaining order in the halls, on the stairways and platforms, and in the neighborhood of the building. The principal shall promptly report to the Supervising Principal all repairs needed, and shall see that the janitor makes all minor repairs without delay and finishes them before the 1st of July. At the close of each school year he shall report to the Supervising Principal what repairs remain undone. All monthly reports and requisitions shall be forwarded through the principal teacher.

31. Teachers shall attend to the physical education and comfort of the pupils under their care, make the ventilation and temperature of the school rooms an especial object of attention, and take care that the windows in the room be opened for the free admission of air at recess, and that the temperature of the rooms shall not fall below 60 nor rise above 70 degrees Fahrenheit. Teachers shall have the temperature, as indicated by a thermometer, observed and recorded on the blackboard three times daily—9 o'clock a. m., 11 o'clock a. m., and 2 o'clock p. m. This should be done by the pupils as far as practicable.

32. They shall practice such discipline in their schools as would be exercised by a kind and judicious parent in the family, always firm and vigilant, but prudent. They shall endeavor, on all proper occasions, to inculcate on their pupils truthfulness, self-control, temperance, frugality, industry, obedience to parents, reverence for the aged, forbearance toward the weak, respect for the rights of others, politeness to all, kindness to animals, desire for knowledge, and obedience to the laws of God; but no teacher shall exercise any sectarian influence in the schools.

33. The avoidance of corporal punishment as far as may be, with a due regard to obedience on the part of pupils, is enjoined on all teachers. Each case of corporal punishment, with the reason therefor, shall be reported monthly by the teacher in charge of the school and forwarded through the Principal or the Supervising Principal to the Superintendent.

34. Teachers shall prevent pupils from sitting too long in one position or without occupation, and shall frequently vary the school exercises, so as to awaken and fix attention. They shall divide their schools when all the pupils are of one grade, into two sections, and shall have one section studying while the other is reciting, as far as may be practicable. In penmanship, drawing, vocal music, and a few other general exercises and explanations the school should be instructed as a whole.

In assigning lessons for study at home the following directions shall be observed:

No lessons shall be assigned to pupils in the First, Second, Third, Fourth or Fifth Grades. The lessons for the pupils of the Sixth or Seventh Grades shall not require more than one hour and a half; of the Eighth

Grade, not more than two hours. Neither arithmetic, penmanship, nor map-drawing shall be assigned for study out of school hours.

In all cases where studies are required at home, the work to be done shall be definitely stated and so thoroughly explained by the teacher that intelligent pupils can master it without assistance in the time prescribed.

35. Teachers shall not be allowed to send their pupils on errands during school hours except on urgent school business.

36. No teacher or other person shall be allowed to present in the Public Schools any premium or gift to any pupil except such as are permitted by order of the board ; nor shall any teacher receive any gift purchased by the contribution of pupils.

37. No person shall be permitted to solicit subscriptions for any paper, book, publication, or other article, or canvass for the sale of any article within the school building at any time, and no subscription for any purpose whatever shall be introduced into any public school, and no advertisement shall be read to the pupils of any school or posted on the walls of any school building or fences of the same without permission of the Board.

38. Teachers are required to make themselves familiar with the rules, especially with the portion that relates to their own duties, and to faithfully observe the same, and to see that the pupils are made familiar with the rules relating to their duties.

SUBSTITUTES.

39. I. In case of the temporary absence of any teacher the Superintendent, or, in cases of emergency, the Supervising Principal, shall promptly provide a substitute, who shall be selected from a list of competent persons to be furnished by the Local Committee, each for his own division, and approved by the Board.

II. The pay of the substitute shall be taken from the salary of the teacher, and for all services in a school where the absence has not aggregated more than thirty (30) days in one school year shall be for each day one-half of one-thirtieth of a month's salary, and for all subsequent continuous service in the same school the substitute, if the holder of a certificate entitling him to teach in that school, shall receive the full salary of the teacher whose place he fills; and if not the holder of such a certificate, such teacher shall receive the highest salary permitted by his (or her) certificate ; or if not the holder of a certificate, then such substitute shall receive the salary of class 1, unless otherwise ordered by the Board : *Provided*, That no substitute shall receive pay for less than a half day's service; and, *provided further*, that all absences shall be reported to the proper Superintendent by the Supervising Principal as soon as ascertained.

SUPERVISING PRINCIPAL.

40. I. The Supervising Principals, as local superintendents of all the schools within their respective divisions, shall under the direction of the Superintendent, be responsible for the observance and enforcement of the rules of the schools, and in the discharge of their duties they shall be entitled to the respect, deference and co-operation of all teachers; and they shall have offices, to be designated by the respective Local Committees, for the transaction of school business.

II. They shall be in their respective offices thirty minutes before the time of the opening each morning session of the schools, and when not engaged in examining schools, under the direction of the Superintendent, from half-past three to four o'clock each afternoon that the schools are in session; and they shall meet at the office of the Superintendent for the purpose of consultation at such times as he may designate.

III. When not engaged in examining schools under the direction of the Superintendent, they shall devote not less than two hours of each school day to teaching in the schools under their charge; and in doing so they shall make it a special object to improve the methods of instruction. They shall make monthly reports of their work to the Superintendent in such form as he may direct.

IV. They shall have a general supervision of the grounds, buildings, furniture, and appurtenances of the schools, and shall see that the same are kept in good condition, and that minor repairs are made by the janitors; they shall see that good order is maintained on school premises and in the neighborhood thereof, and that the strictest cleanliness is maintained in the school buildings and out-houses belonging thereto; they shall promptly report to their respective Local Committees any repairs that may be required and any negligence of the janitors; they shall make requisition on the Superintendent for all supplies of fuel, books, stationery and other articles required for the use of the schools, and they shall see that books, slates, and other articles are loaned only to those pupils whose parents or guardians are actually not able to furnish the same by reason of indigence, and that all books, slates, or other articles so loaned are returned to their offices at the close of each school year.

V. They shall keep, according to forms approved by the Board, a correct account of all supplies received by them, and of all supplies distributed to the schools; and they shall keep an accurate record of the names of all pupils suspended or dismissed from the schools, noting in each case the date, the offense committed, and any other particulars which may be deemed important. These accounts and records shall be at all times open to the inspection of the Trustees and the Superintendent.

VI. They shall furnish, according to the prescribed form, the Superintendent with the required monthly and annual reports of the schools and monthly lists of the names of all teachers and janitors employed by the

Board, and the amount of salary due to each; and they shall furnish such other information as may be required from time to time by the trustees and the Superintendent.

VII. They shall see that the teachers are promptly notified and duly advised as to all rules and orders pertaining to the schools, and that they carry out the same in every particular; they shall see that all the prescribed records are neatly, regularly, and accurately kept by the teachers, and that all reports and returns required by the Board or the Superintendent are promptly made; they shall, under the direction of the Superintendent, classify the pupils in the different grades according to the course of study; they shall visit each school as often as practicable; and they shall in every way possible, co-operate with the Superintentent in advising teachers as to the best methods of instructing and governing their schools.

SCHOOL YEAR AND SESSIONS.

41. I. The school year shall commence on the first day of July of each year, and shall end on the last day of the following June.

II. The schools shall be in session on all the week days of the school year, except the following:

Every Saturday.

From the Thursday falling between the 18th and 24th of June, inclusive, until the Friday before the Monday falling between the 17th and 23d of the following September, inclusive.

Thanksgiving day and the following Friday.

From the day before Christmas Day until New Year's Day, both inclusive; and when the second day of January is observed as New Year's Day, it shall be included; and when New Year's Day falls on Thursday, the following Friday shall be included.

Washington's Birthday, and, when it falls on Thursday, the following Friday shall be included.

Good Friday and Easter Monday.

III. In emergencies the schools may be closed by order of the President of the Board of Trustees upon other days not to exceed three days in any one year.

IV. No other holidays shall be granted without the formal consent of the Board of Trustees.

V. The City Schools from the Third to the Eighth Grade, both inclusive, and the County Schools shall be opened at 9 o'clock a. m., and shall be closed at 3 o'clock p. m., punctually. A recess of fifteen minutes shall be given at 10½ o'clock a. m., and one of sixty minutes at 12 m., but on stormy days the noon recess may be dispensed with by permission of the Supervising Principal, and in the latter case the schools shall be closed at 1 o'clock.

VI. In all City Schools and such County Schools as may be designated by the Committee on Teachers and Janitors, upon the recommendation of the Superintendent and the Local Committee, the daily sessions shall be for the First Grade Schools, not exceeding three-and-a-half hours; for Second Grade Schools, not exceeding four hours; and a recess of fifteen minutes shall be given in the middle of each session.

EXAMINATIONS.

42. Examinations of the several schools shall be made from time to time by the Supervising Principals under the direction of the Superintendents, and all pupils absenting themselves from such examination, without cause assigned, shall be reported in writing to the Superintendent, and may be suspended or dismissed by the same.

SCHOOL HOUSES.

43. The Trustees are responsible for the proper use of the public property intrusted to their care, and the school-houses shall be used only for Public School purposes.

JANITORS.

44. Each Janitor shall be subject to the order of the Principal and of the other Executive Officers. He shall be responsible for all damage done through his neglect or carelessness. He shall make and regulate the fires; notify the Principal in season when fuel is needed; preserve the heating apparatus; sweep, dust, and wash the rooms, halls, and windows as often as is necessary, or when so directed by the Principal; keep the out-houses clean and in good order at all times; keep the playgrounds and grass plats in a cleanly condition; guard the buildings, furniture, fences and grounds; see that the windows, shutters, doors and gates are securely fastened when the schools are not in session; receipt for all materials delivered for minor repairs, and keep a faithful record of the same and of the use made of them; promptly make such repairs as he is able to make, and report to the Principal all other repairs needed, and do such other work as properly belongs to the janitor—such as washing and filling ink-wells, providing water for the use of teachers and pupils, assisting in maintaining order outside the building, and going on official errands for the Principal when the heating apparatus is not in use: *Provided*, That some competent person be at all times left in charge of the building. The janitor of a steam or furnace-heated building shall not be absent under any circumstances during school hours when the heating apparatus is in use. A janitor may be required to labor on minor repairs, whenever he shall be most needed in or about any school building in the District, provided his services are not required in the building of which he has special charge. No firemen, sweep, or other assistant to a janitor shall be employed or discharged without the written approval of the Local Committee of the division. All janitors shall be paid on monthly pay-rolls.

BOOKS AND FORMS.

45. All officers of the Board and teachers shall use such record and other blank books and such forms as shall be prescribed by the Board and in the manner and for the purpose designated; and the instructions accompanying such books and forms are hereby made a part of the rules. In each school-room a copy of the rules shall be kept by the teacher.

APPEALS.

46. The Executive Officers of the Board shall rank in the following order: Teachers, Principals, Supervising Principals, Superintendents and Local Committees. Appeals may be taken from the decision of any of these officers to the next higher rank, and from the Local Committees to the Board. Pending any appeal the decision must be obeyed.

NOMENCLATURE.

47. The following system of names shall be used in all the reports and records of the Public Schools, to wit: First, the grade of the school shall be given, together with the number of the school, if there be more than one school of the grade of the same sex, in the same building; second the sex of pupils attending such school; third, the name of the school. Example: Fourth Grade, boys, Henry School, or, Fourth Grade, No. 1, boys, Henry School. The Superintendent is charged with the enforcement of this rule.

NORMAL SCHOOLS.

48. The following rules are prescribed for the Normal Schools:

I. The number of pupils in the Washington Normal School shall be limited to fifty, of whom ten may be male; and the number in the Normal School of the Seventh and Eighth divisions shall be limited to twenty-six, all of whom shall be selected from graduates of the respective high schools.

II. Each candidate must not be less than eighteen years of age; and before being admitted must pass an examination, to be conducted by the Committee on Normal and High Schools, equivalent to that upon which teachers' Fourth Class certificates are issued.

III. An annual examination of candidates shall be held in the month of June; and the Committee shall issue tickets of admission to those found qualified (not exceeding fifty in number for the Washington Normal School, and twenty-six for the Normal School of the Seventh and Eighth divisions) commencing with the one who stands highest in scholarship, and continuing in the order of their rank.

IV. Each candidate, before being admitted to the school shall be required to sign the following pledge: " I, the subscriber, desire to enter the Normal School, for the sole purpose of better preparing myself for the business of teaching; and I declare it to be my intention to continue in said school until I have completed the prescribed course of study, and then to devote myself to the work of teaching in the public schools of the District for a period of at least two years. In witness whereof I have hereunto subscribed my name."

V. The course of study shall be strictly professional.

VI. All text-books, books of reference, maps, charts, apparatus, etc., used by the schools shall be furnished by the Board.

VII. Each graduate shall receive a certificate, on which shall be stated the rank of the recipient, and this certificate shall be equivalent to a Fourth Class Certificate, and shall be good for one year. Graduates from the Normal School who have taught in the public schools of the District not less than one year, and given satisfactory evidence of their ability to govern and instruct a school, shall be entitled to receive diplomas, which shall be equivalent to Fourth Class Certificates.

VIII. The studies shall be pursued with special reference to the best methods of teaching.

TRAINING SCHOOLS.

49. I. The Committee on Normal and High Schools shall designate one or more of the Public Schools of the District as Training Schools, wherein the pupil-teachers of the Normal Schools may learn, by observation and practice, methods of governing and instructing children.

II. The training Schools shall be detached from the "practical supervision" of the Local Committees of the divisions in which they may be located, and shall be in charge of the Committee on Normal and High Schools.

www.ingramcontent.com/pod-product-compliance
Lightning Source LLC
Chambersburg PA
CBHW021818230426
43669CB00008B/789